THE CAMBRIDGE SEVEN

THE CAMBRIDGE SEVEN

John Pollock

Centenary Edition

Marshalls

Marshalls Paperbacks
Marshall Morgan & Scott
3 Beggarwood Lane, Basingstoke, Hants, RG23 7LP, UK

First published in 1955 by IVP, this revised edition first
co-published by Marshall Pickering Ltd and OMF Books
in 1985

British Library CIP data

Pollock, J. C.
   The Cambridge Seven. – 2nd ed.
   1. Church of England – History   2. Cambridge
   (Cambridgeshire) – Church history
   I. Title
   283'.42659   BX5105.C3

   ISBN 0-551-01174-2

Reproduced, printed and bound in Great Britain by
Hazell Watson & Viney Limited,
Member of the BPCC Group,
Aylesbury, Bucks

CONTENTS

BIOGRAPHICAL NOTES

BEAUCHAMP, MONTAGU HARRY PROCTOR-, *born* 19th April, 1860, 4th son of Sir Thomas Proctor-Beauchamp, 4th Bt. (d. 1874) and the Hon. Caroline Waldegrave (yst. daughter of 2nd Lord Radstock), of Langley Park, Norfolk, and 3 Cromwell Road, London, S. W. *Educ.* Repton School and Trinity College, Cambridge (Matric. 1879, B.A. 1883), Ridley Hall 1883.

CASSELS, WILLIAM WHARTON, *born* 11th March, 1859, yst son of John Cassels, of Oporto, Portugal (d. 1869) and Ethelinda Cox. *Educ.* Repton School and St. John's College, Cambridge (Matric. 1877, B.A. 1880). Ordained deacon 1882, priest 1883. Curate of All Saints, South Lambeth 1882-4.

HOSTE, DIXON EDWARD, *born* 23rd July, 1861, 2nd son of Major-General Dixon Edward Hoste and Mary Scott, of Havelock Lodge, Brighton. *Educ.* Clifton College and Royal Military Academy, Woolwich. 2nd Lieut., Royal Artillery 1879, Lieut. 1882.

POLHILL-TURNER, ARTHUR TWISTLETON, *born* 7th February, 1863, 3rd son of Capt. Frederick Charles Polhill-Turner, D. L., J. P., M. P. (d. 1881) and Emily Winston Barron, of Howbury Hall, Bedford,. *Educ.* Eton College and Trinity Hall, Cambridge (Matric. 1880, B. A. 1884), Ridley Hall 1884.

POLHILL-TURNER, CECIL HENRY, *born* 23rd February, 1860, 2nd son of Capt. Polhill-Turner (above). *Educ.* Eton College and Jesus College,

Cambridge (Matric. 1879). 2nd Lieut., Bedford-shire Yeomanry 1880, 2nd Lieut., 2nd Dragoon Guards (The Queen's Bays) 1881, Lieut. 1884.

SMITH, STANLEY PEREGRINE, *born* 19thMarch, 1861, yst. son of Henry Smith, F.R.C.S. and Alice Underwood, of 13 John Street, Berkeley Square, London, W. *Educ.* Repton School and Trinity College, Cambridge (Matric. 1879, B. A. 1882).

STUDD, CHARLES THOMAS, *born* 2nd December, 1860, 3rd son of Edward Studd (d. 1877) and Dorothy Thomas, of Tedworth House, Wiltshire, and 2 Hyde Park Gardens, London, W. *Educ.* Eton College and Trinity College, Cambridge (Matric. 1879, B. A. 1884).

PROLOGUE

Early in 1885, on a wet winter's night in London, the Strand was crowded with carriages and hansom cabs converging on Exeter Hall.

The 'large room' holding three thousand was filling rapidly with men and women of all ages and ranks. Ladies in silks and jewelry, whose carriages waited to carry them back to Belgravia or Mayfair, mingled with flower-girls and working women in plain dark dresses who had found their way on foot from East End slums. Smart young city men were sitting beside drab shopmen and kindly rogues who, on a superficial glance, might have seemed more at home in a music hall.

On the platform sat forty Cambridge undergraduates. Above their heads hung a large map of China, stretching from side to side. On the table lay a small pile of Chinese New Testaments.

At the stroke of the hour the Chairman entered, followed by seven young men slightly older than the undergraduates but all, from their dress and bearing, men of education and position. After prayer, a hymn, and some introductory remarks those, whom the world had already dubbed the Cambridge Seven rose in turn to tell the crowded hall why they were leaving England the next day to serve as missionaries in inland China.

One by one they spoke – Stanley Smith, of

Repton and Trinity, a former stroke of the Cambridge boat; Montagu Beauchamp of Trinity, a baronet's son; D. E. Hoste, till lately a gunner subaltern, son of a major-general; W .W. Cassels of Repton and St. John's, a Church of England curate. Then came Cecil Polhill-Turner, an Old Etonian, who had resigned his commission in the Queen's Bays (2nd Dragoon Guards) to join the others; and his brother Arthur, of Eton and Trinity Hall. And lastly C.T. Studd, the Eton, Cambridge and England cricketer, acknowledged as the most brilliant player of the day. One by one they told how in the past year or eighteen months God had called them to renounce their careers and give themselves for Christian service overseas.

The Cambridge Seven struck with force the consciousness of a generation which set much store on social position and athletic ability. A century later the story of how the Seven was formed is still relevant. Any account of God's working on the human soul is timeless, but the Cambridge Seven provide particular evidence about growth in grace and on God's calling to full-time service. Furthermore, the events of 1885 had a formative influence on the history of missions, and of Christian work in universities throughout the world.

The Cambridge Seven emerged when Britain had been stirred to the depths by the work of D. L. Moody, the American evangelist. Seventy years later, when this book was first published in 1955, Cambridge University and all Britain were being stirred by the work of another American evangelist, Billy Graham. Yet again, thirty years on, the Centenary of the Cambridge Seven follows the great meetings of Mission England when thousands of young men and women were among the nearly ninety-seven thousand people in England who responded to Billy Graham's call for commitment to Christ.

Thus a reissue of this book is timely. I have rewritten parts and have introduced several contemporary letters which were not available in 1955. I am very grateful to the Overseas Missionary Fellowship, as the China Inland Mission has become, for allowing me to publish them, and especially to Dr. A. J. Broomhall, former C.I.M. – O.M.F. missionary, who is writing the definitive life of its founder, Hudson Taylor, for researching them for me in the archives, and for Dr. Broomhall's advice and theirs.

In the Prologue of the first edition I wrote: 'If China is again a closed land, though not now without its Christian witness, other lands are open, and fields at home are waiting.' At that time, three years after the withdrawal of all but a beleaguered handful of western missionaries, it almost seemed that Hudson Taylor, the Cambridge Seven and their thousands of fellow-workers had achieved comparatively little by their devotion and sacrifice.

Thirty years later, in the Centenary year of the Seven, the world knows that the Christian church in China has not only survived but grown beyond all measure.

Chapter 1

TRINITY FRESHMAN

Stanley Peregrine Smith was a slight, fair haired youth, with a determined little mouth, when he entered Trinity College, Cambridge in October 1879. Aged eighteen and a half he had not come up straight from school like most of the freshmen, for a serious illness had obliged him to leave Repton early. He had enjoyed a year of convalescence and freedom.

Smith came from a home which was quietly but unashamedly Christian. His father, a successful London surgeon, had thought nothing of kneeling in prayer with the boy after settling him into his rooms in Market Passage under the shadow of Great St. Mary's. Stanley himself had 'accepted the Saviour' (his own phrase) at the age of thirteen in 1874, while listening at Eastbourne to D. L. Moody, the American evangelist who had stirred all Scotland and was preaching in the English provinces before starting in London. At Repton Stanley had joined a little meeting for prayer and Bible study formed by an older boy, Granville Waldegrave, in a room over the tuck-shop, and he wanted to be a Church of England parson; yet by 1879 his religion had become an ineffective struggle to live up to good intentions.

He kept a diary describing each day – a little work, much skating during that hard, prolonged winter of 1878-9, the exciting new game of lawn tennis during the summer, and boating, bathing or bicycling on the fifty-two inch Singer penny-farthing with steel-plated hubs and rims, a gift from his father and the pride of his life; but, he could find nothing to say about his spiritual life except 'poor', 'unsatisfactory,' 'very poor,' 'a little wee improvement,' 'character un-Christlike and foolish.'

Moreover he suffered from colds, chills and sore chests, a legacy of his illness; and as he saw no connection between physical ill-health and spiritual decay, and gauged his faith by his feelings, the reports were generally bad.

All this went little further than his diary. His family and friends knew him as an affectionate, happy-natured boy with a strong sense of humour, who might be a little argumentative and contradictory and have phases of moody nervousness, yet never complained of his ills and was remarkably plucky in sticking to games and work despite frequent pain. But Stanley Smith was a defeated Christian and he knew it.

The first weeks at Cambridge passed in a whirl. Smith was soon down at the river, though not having rowed for a year he was placed in one of the lowest boats. He was elected a member of the Bicycle Club and pedalled happily on his penny-farthing to Grantchester and the Gogs. Repton friends were all around, especially Montagu Beauchamp, of tall, athletic build, a year older than Smith but closest at school, who had also come up to Trinity. They were in and out of each other's rooms and walked together in cap and gown through Old Court (now Great Court) to dine in Hall.

Beauchamp's parents, Sir Thomas, who had died five years before, and Lady Beauchamp, a sister of Lord Radstock the noted evangelist, had made Langley Park their Norfolk home, a centre of Christian activity. Smith and Beauchamp thus had much in common. They would go occasionally to the Daily Prayer Meeting in the hired room above All Saints' Passage and to the weekly meeting on Sundays of the recently formed Inter-Collegiate Christian Union, and help at a Sunday School in the slums. In their own rooms they would try to recapture the atmosphere of the Repton tuck-shop meetings.

On the river Smith met again another Old Reptonian, William Cassels of St. John's, a good footballer and moderate oarsman, who was reading for Holy Orders. A quiet, reserved man, dubbed 'William the Silent,' he was already in his third year. Neither etiquette nor inclination drew them much together.

Cambridge undergraduates in 1879 were almost all from public schools or the larger grammar schools and exclusively male: women had just been admitted to lectures but could not take degrees. Stanley Smith made friends easily with Trinity freshmen from other schools, and in particular with William Hoste, up from Clifton College, who was both a Christian and a rowing man. Once Smith met Willie's younger brother, D.E. Hoste, a shy and taciturn gunner subaltern very recently commissioned, and entirely uninterested in Christian gossip.

Beauchamp introduced Smith to an Old Etonian in his second year named G. B. Studd, already prominent as a cricketer. His younger brother, C. T. Studd was even better at the game, a freshman who seemed to live only for cricket, in season and out. Their father, a retired Indian planter who had recently died, had been converted in the Moody and Sankey London mission of 1875, so the Studds enjoyed Christian chatter and were always ready to have a few 'Sankeys' round the piano and a prayer or two to follow.

'C. T.', Smith and Beauchamp, with Cassels the intending parson and D. E. Hoste the gunner would have all been astounded had they seen their future.

As Stanley Smith's first term advanced, rowing took more of his time. He entered for the freshmen's sculls, despite his chest which disliked the Cambridge damp, and was defeated in the final; but found himself to his great delight chosen stroke of First Trinity freshmen's eight. The scramble to keep lectures, get to the river, and put in a few hours' reading and the customary amount of idle lounging or singing with friends meant the occasional loss of his 'half-hour,' the daily time of Bible reading and prayer on his own. He would make up his losses by sitting before an open Bible on a Sunday, trying to keep thoughts from wandering too far.

During his second term he cut the Daily Prayer Meeting and frequently forgot Sunday School, though not his 'half-hour.' In the Lent Races he rowed in First Trinity's sixth boat, which ('rather bad luck') was bumped every day. He sang and danced his way through the end of term celebrations and was then home again, a day before his nineteenth birthday, for the Easter vacation and plenty of lawn tennis in the fine March weather. The 'half-hour' of Bible reading was dropping off; but deep in his heart he was unhappy.

On 8th April, 1880, the Honourable Granville Waldegrave, the Old Reptonian who had formed the tuck-shop meeting four years before, called on Stanley Smith at 13 John Street, Mayfair.

Waldegrave, Lord Radstock's eldest son and Monty Beauchamp's first cousin, was a Trinity undergraduate in his second year, but he had been in Russia with his father, who had conducted a remarkably successful evangelistic mission among the Princesses and Grand Dukes of the Court at St. Petersburg. He had missed Stanley's first two terms. Waldegrave had never ceased to pray for him, and for three and a half hours the two friends walked the London pavements and Regent's Park. Smith was obliged, grudgingly enough, to admit to Waldegrave that he was no longer too heartfelt a Christian.

The next day was all lawn tennis down at Twickenham, where Stanley's eldest brother Ernest was in practice as a doctor. On the Saturday Waldegrave, Beauchamp and Smith travelled up to Cambridge together. Waldegrave was biding his time.

Sunday, 11th April, began ordinarily enough. Smith yawned his way through the Trinity Chapel service, and afterwards Beauchamp suggested breakfast in his rooms, asking Waldegrave too. During the porridge, fish, eggs and bacon and hot rolls which the kitchens had sent up, Waldegrave watched for his opportunity. The conversation turned casually, as it often did, to Christian matters. Waldegrave did not allow it to remain casual. Soon the three of them were deep in talk. At midday they crossed to Market Passage for lunch in Smith's rooms. Smith sat at the piano and played and sang hymns in his fine voice and they read a passage together. For Beauchamp this informal talk on an April Sunday was just one of many. But for Smith it began a new era.

Nearly six years earlier, listening to D. L. Moody, Stanley Smith had realized that Christ had died on the Cross, 'the just for the unjust that he might bring us to God,' and that every man was called to a personal trust in the risen Saviour, to open the heart to His Spirit. As Smith later wrote, 'I was by grace enabled to receive Christ.' Nothing in time or eternity could destroy the reality of the new birth nor separate Smith 'from the love of God, which is in Christ Jesus our Lord'; but the carefree response of a boy of thirteen to his Saviour had weakened with the years. He had surrendered all his life to Christ in 1874; by 1880 he had taken much of it back. Thus he now served two masters. At heart self-centred, he could not forget that tribute was due, though grudged, to his Redeemer.

Waldegrave, while Beauchamp listened, showed Smith that though Christ had promised, 'I will never leave thee nor forsake thee', His spirit could not restore the joy of His salvation nor give strength in temptation until Smith yielded Him all – mind, will, emotions, activities. It was no use pledging more to God; Stanley must give all without reserve, even as God in Christ had given Himself for Stanley.

Stanley's eyes were opened. 'I decided,' as he wrote that evening, 'by God's grace to live by and for Him.' And because Waldegrave, and Smith's parents, were praying and Stanley was repentant and humble, God took him at his word.

The result was marked. After chapel the three of them went to Waldegrave's rooms for tea 'and had another delightful meeting. Thank God for sending G.W. here.' Before going to bed Smith hurried round to Willie Hoste to tell him what had happened. In the days that followed Smith felt weak enough but Waldegrave was there to help. For the first weeks they met two or three times a day for brief periods of Bible reading and prayer, which Smith found he 'enjoyed immensely'. He bought a little pocket Bible. The dreary 'half-hours' which had dogged him were transformed into exciting voyages of discovery in a Book which seemed alive. When a bilious attack came he found to his surprise that he no longer grew depressed.

In work and sport the faraway Christ, whom he had tried not to displease, now proved a Friend at his side. Smith had been promoted stroke of the fourth boat. His weak chest made training hard, but the May Races were thoroughly enjoyable and on the last day 'to my great delight we bumped Catherine's, a little way down the Long Reach. The only bump Trinity made, I am thankful to God for it, as He alone gave me strength.'

Early in the long vacation he felt spiritually insecure again. Then at a conference in North London he met Edward Clifford, the fashionable portrait painter who soon would be closely involved in the founding of the Church Army. Clifford saw at once that this young Cambridge man with his eager yet hesitant faith needed some open service for Christ,and took him to a mission hall in the slums of the East End where F.N. Charrington, a brewer's son who had sacrificed a fortune and shocked society by turning teetotal, had founded a temperance mission outside the family brewery in Stepney.

For the first time, Stanley prayed extempore in public. The next day he preached, also for the first time, at Clifford's open-air meeting on the waste ground behind the Temperance Hall. A crowded fortnight began, speaking, listening, tract-giving and praying, interspersed with lawn tennis with his family, a 'scrumptious' bicycle ride on the new wooden paving of Park Lane and a picnic on the river in pouring rain.

The thrill of Christian service was on him. As Smith heard Lord Radstock, Clifford or Charrington call men forward to give their lives to Christ, he would be praying with all his might that 'souls may be born again.' He knew for certain that his vocation lay in such work. His heart went out to the poor, the ragged, the drunkards. He became teetotal and gave up smoking, a more unusual step at that time when the connection between smoking and damage to health had not been discovered.

Slumming and open-air preaching were no sacrifice; his colleagues were of his own class or higher – Clifford, Radstock, Lord Kintore, Abel Smith the M.P. If it meant late nights, it was the servants at

John Street who suffered, as Stanley was late for breakfast. Charrington, his hero, then persuaded him to submit to believers' baptism, against the wishes of his family and his prospects of ordination as an Anglican clergyman.

Two days later Clifford took him to Aldershot for work at Miss Daniell's Soldiers' Home. If Stepney had given him a taste of Christian service, Aldershot showed him the wonder of bringing men to Christ. Speaking came naturally, and to see five or six soldiers respond to his call 'to decide for the Lord', and to receive a scrawled letter a few days later from a private of Rifles, 'thanking me as being the means of his conversion,' filled the cup of his joy.

His faith blazed up. It seemed almost too easy. The days passed in a stream of open-airs, teas, hospital visits, and country house conferences for deepening of spiritual life.

A new sacrifice lay at hand. Stanley felt more strongly every day that he should throw up Cambridge and go abroad at once as a missionary. He had no particular area in mind. Beauchamp had sometimes spoken of the China Inland Mission, a recent pioneering venture led by a Yorkshireman, Hudson Taylor, of which Sir Thomas and Lady Beauchamp had been among the earliest supporters. But Stanley Smith's thoughts were not directed towards China or elsewhere so much as to the vital need to win souls. The sooner he was out the more he could win. 'O Lord,' he wrote in his diary, 'save souls and lay upon me the burden of souls, at least twenty-five thousand.' To continue education, he presumed, was a waste of time.

Early in September he wrote to his parents, from Derbyshire where he was staying with cousins, for their sanction. The Smiths were wise and prayerful. They did not write back a peremptory refusal, but they urged caution. Stanley's first reaction was to believe that prayer would prevail to convince them, but soon he was worried as to the right course, and some of the old depressions came back.

He threw himself into evangelistic work among the cottagers, stifling spiritual uncertainties by unstinting activity. With one of the cousins he spent a night in prayer, at the price of feeling 'very seedy' later in the morning. On another night, long hours' praying for faith brought glorious but short-lived ecstasy. The two young men even sent a letter to Mr. Mello, the local rector, 'to awaken Mr. M. to his sense of responsibility,' and shook their heads sadly at his reply, 'full, I am afraid, of lame excuses and not owning one bit to his lack of energy for the Master.'

As the new Cambridge term approached, S. P. Smith remained uncertain of God's will and humbly desired guidance. He was taken at his word. On 6th October the allotted chapter in his daily Bible reading was the third chapter of Ezekiel. As he read, Ezekiel 3.5 seemed to strike out as a clear message from his Lord: 'For thou art not sent to a people of a strange speech and of an hard language, but to the house of Israel'.

As he pondered, he became clear in his mind that God was not calling him, as he had supposed, to the mission field but to service at home. And that meant remaining at Cambridge until his undergraduate course was done. What is more, reading

22

and discussion with older friends convinced him that he had been wrong to rush into believers' baptism as binding on all Christians. He could be an Anglican parson with a good conscience.

It was therefore a chastened and humble S. P. Smith who began his second year at Cambridge. But 'when I look back on the year past I see nothing but a *continued stream* of mercies.'

Chapter 2

CAMBRIDGE BLUE

A third Studd had come up to Trinity as a freshman
– the eldest, Kynaston, who had been in business.
Like his younger brothers, J. E. K. Studd was a fine
cricketer; but whereas G. B. and C. T. put Christ
last of their loyalties, J. E. K. had a strong sense of
service. Smith was drawn to him at once, and soon
learned to value his age and experience. He became
a closer friend than either William Hoste or
Beauchamp, with their casual Christianity which
Smith had left behind.

Monty Beauchamp, the third son in a large
family, had always lived in an atmosphere of
Christian activity and unpretentious devotion.
One of his earliest memories, as a boy of five, was
Hudson Taylor's visit soon after he had founded
the China Inland Mission. Taylor and his missionaries wore Chinese dress and pigtails when on the
field (at the price of Westerners' contempt) and
thus could go where others could not. Monty remembered Hudson Taylor showing the children
chopsticks and a pigtail and other curiosities and
telling them of the millions who knew nothing of
the Lord Jesus.

As the Beauchamp family grew up each of the
sisters adopted particular Christian concerns, and
sometimes Monty would join Ida's meetings for

London policemen, or go with Hilda round the flower girls. Lord Radstock was his favourite uncle, and he was always ready to hear him preach. Yet somehow, year by year, Monty had remained a formal, stunted Christian.

During the Christmas vacation the three Studds, Smith and Beauchamp frequently skated together on the frozen Serpentine in Hyde Park. Next term, early in February 1881, Smith and Beauchamp were helping Kynaston Studd hang pictures in his Cambridge rooms. Monty, not feeling too well, left early for bed. After the pictures were hung, Smith and Studd had a brief prayer. As they rose from their knees Studd asked Smith if he would 'come and pray for Beauchamp every day'. Smith, recalling Beauchamp's lukewarm faith, his occasional tempers, his stunted spiritual growth in such contrast to physical height and strength, and realizing afresh how fond he was of his Repton friend, readily agreed. They decided to meet for a quarter of an hour each evening after hall.

Smith then suggested that they should 'form a little society, the object being to speak to at least one unconverted soul (who must be an undergraduate) a month'. Studd accepted wholeheartedly and, a few days later, Waldergrave. On 28th February William Gallwey, a Reptonian who had been a freshman with Smith, 'gave his heart to Jesus – answer to four months' prayer', and the next day, after they had read *Romans 5* together, Smith was thrilled to join Gallwey's first faltering extempore prayer, 'I thank Thee God that at last I can accept Thy gift of eternal life.' Gallwey, son of a soldier and grandson of an archdeacon, was ordained in 1883 and spent a lifetime in parish work.

When Smith won the Macnaghten Sculls by twenty yards, despite his health, he used the prize money to buy a copy of Holman Hunt's picture *The Light of the World* as an aid to evangelism. Rowing, however, began subtly to choke Smith's spiritual life. Academic work was not too demanding but the river, which would later contribute so much to his great appeal to contemporaries, became a danger, partly because all his rowing exploits were achieved with a weak chest.

He won the University pairs ('It is fine beating these Varsity oars') and his boat did well in the Mays; but even the hour of quiet prayer and Bible reading was dropping off, and the teetotal fervour of the previous summer was drowned, temperately enough, in Henley champagne. By the end of June he was realizing that 'my soul is in a wretchedly poor state.' He did not go near Stepney or Aldershot in the Long Vacation and when he visited the Derbyshire cousins there was more tennis than tracts; the worthy rector might have supposed that he had the last laugh.

Decline was more apparent than real. On 1st August Smith recorded in his diary, 'Got up at 7 and for the first time for some months started the day really well with nice prayer. What a difference it makes.' Soon afterwards he wrote out a list of all his friends and Christian activities and saw to it that he remembered regularly each name. Yet if Smith was too deep to fall away, he might drift into respectable, earnest but unsacrificial service, a moderate-minded parson, orthodox but not evangelistic, like so many clergy of the day.

The Michaelmas term began, and the pendulum swung back. If the previous October had sobered, that of 1881 revitalized him as he picked up the threads of Christian Union friendships and activities. 'Oh, God,' he wrote after reading from Isaiah with two others, 'I do seem to have fallen away so. Restore me, for Jesus sake. Let not the world or worldly honours draw me away from Thee.'

S. P. Smith was now Captain of First Trinity Boat Club and thus a man of influence in the college, with a good chance of his blue. The routine duty of recruiting freshmen for the boats gave him a new idea. In his rooms in Old Court, looking across the wide lawn to the fountain and the clock tower, he and two of the others sat down to write out a list of the freshmen 'with a view to visiting them and trying by all means to do them good. C. T. Studd came in. We had singing, reading and prayer and I asked him to take some men. Altogether it was a delightful evening.'

William Cassels, now a bachelor of arts reading for his deacon's examination, was a strong support. The disparity of age seemed less, and the eager, active Smith was increasingly drawn to the silent, gentle Cassels. Cassels had no academic distinction; he had missed his soccer blue through a broken leg. But he was set for a steady career of selfless Christian service.

The best of all was a 'scrumptious' letter from Kynaston Studd, who was coming up late, enclosing another from Montagu Beauchamp telling Studd that he had at last 'yielded all to Christ.' When Monty came up, 'How marvellously changed he is!' wrote Smith, 'so full of zeal instead of his coldness and luke-warmness.' Together they decided to start a Bible reading group for members of First Trinity Boat Club.

Smith's spiritual life swung backwards and forwards. He and Beauchamp both rowed in the trial eights at Ely, though Smith was far from fit. Beauchamp was growing steadily but during the Christmas vacation Smith started smoking again and when he crossed the Channel in January 1882 to stay with Lady Beauchamp and her family and her Waldegrave nephews and nieces, at Honfleur in Normandy, it was Monty who took the lead and drew Stanley back.

They spent a happy fortnight evangelizing *en famille* the ships and fishermen, improving their French more than the souls of their hearers. The one disappointment, for Smith, was that Beauchamp had received a summons to the Varsity boat and Smith had not. But when he returned to London the summons was awaiting him, and during the course of the Lent term it was Beauchamp, rowing fifth, who lost his place ('how wonderfully he is bearing it,' commented Smith) and Smith who was confirmed as stroke of the Varsity boat and given his blue.

Smith was known throughout Cambridge as a Christian (at Oxford, which he visited in March, the irrepressible 'Frisky Frank' Webster introduced him as a 'Hallelujah Stroke') and his position as a Varsity oar and his charm of manner enabled him to speak directly to his contemporaries on their spiritual need. He determined to approach every man in the University Boat. 'May the whole eight be Christians,' was his prayer. Monty Beauchamp worked so effectively on the Trial boat that its tee-total tendency earned it the nickname, 'Teapot eight'.

The Boat Race of 1882 was lost dismally to Oxford by seven lengths. Smith's reputation was un-tarnished and he was now considered one of the outstanding oarsmen of the day; sheer grit and determination had overcome his earlier physical weakness and slow start. However, 'I'm afraid my soul has suffered a good deal during the training for the Boat Race,' and he was inclined to be gloomy and low throughout the Easter vacation. Returning to Cambridge for his last term revived him, and after a talk with Hoste he resolved, finally and, as it proved, permanently to abjure smoking 'and by God's grace, provided it does not injure health, alcoholic drinks.'

Early in June came the May Races, in which Trinity failed to break Jesus' run as Head of the River. On 17th June 1882, Smith took his degree, and with the Henley Regatta and all its excitement his Cambridge career came to a close in a blaze of glory.

Not now certain that he wished to be ordained, he arranged to start in September under his brother-in-law, Lloyd Griffith, who owned a pre-paratory school in South London, preparing small boys for entry into public schools. This would be temporary, while he decided what to do.

Chapter 3

THE BROTHERS

In the little village of Ravensden on the edge of the
Ouse valley near Bedford, one warm winter's day
in the early eighteen-seventies, an old widow
stood at the door of her little cottage to watch the
hounds go by as the hunt moved off from the
nearby meet. Mrs. Symons' face was as bright as
the brass knocker which was the pride of her
cottage, and if she was poor she was happy. She
waved to the huntsman in his pink coat and
bobbed a little curtsy to the Master, and to her
Squire and his lady, and waved merrily to the chat-
tering children on their ponies, who waved back.
There were plenty of children, some on leading-
reins, others riding proudly by themselves. But as
she watched she was especially struck by one
family which she had often seen before – the
sons and daughters of Captain Polhill-Turner of
Howbury Hall. Back at her fireside the old woman
felt certain that her Saviour, her constant Companion in the lonely cottage, was calling her to pray
for those children. And since Mrs. Symons was
accustomed to obey her Master she responded
promptly, and continued day by day to remember
them in prayer.

The Polhill children (the additional name of

Turner was added when their mother inherited a fortune) had been born and bred at Howbury, a typical eighteenth-century country house set in a park to the north of the road leading eastwards from Bedford. The three boys and three girls had all that they needed – hunting and amateur theatricals in the winter, cricket and boating in the summer with friends of their own age from neighbouring houses. Their father, to whom they were devoted, was Member of Parliament for Bedford, and High Sheriff for the county in '75.

Cecil and Arthur, the second and third sons, were closest to one another and in due course went to Eton. Their careers were already planned according to the custom of the day. Frederick, the eldest, would inherit. Cecil, as second, would enter the cavalry and Arthur would be ordained and take the family living. Arthur's views on religion were hazy enough, despite the wonderful stories told at bedtime in nursery days by their Nannie, Readshaw, who talked as if Jesus Christ was her personal friend; but he presumed he would acquire the necessary learning at Cambridge, and no doubt would enjoy a pleasant and worthy life as a country rector.

Eton days could scarcely have been happier. Arthur won his house colours for football while still a lower boy, Cecil played for the school in the Field Game in 1877 and was two years in the cricket eleven. Arthur received his cricket colours in '79 from the great C. T. Studd and, after Cecil had gone up to Jesus College, Cambridge, in preparation for the Army, had two further years in the Eton cricket and football elevens, and one as Keeper of the

Field. The two boys were both small and stocky, Cecil quiet and dogged, Arthur jolly and quick to make friends

Only two shocks disturbed their even lives. The first, of short duration, was the sudden announcement by their elder sister Alice that she was going to renounce the world, and give up hunting and parties, to serve Christ. Unaware of those who were praying for her she had quietly made the discovery of her spiritual need through reading the Bible, and at a mission service in Bedford had taken Christ as her Saviour. Cecil and Arthur considered her subsequent efforts on behalf of their souls a tiresome disturbance, but she soon left them alone. Her odd decision was the talk of the hunting field that winter.

The second shock was severe. During Arthur's last half at Eton, when Cecil had just received his commission in the Queen's Bays (2nd Dragoon Guards) their father died at the early age of fifty-five.

Under the shadow of Captain Polhill-Turner's, death Cecil joined his regiment in Ireland and Arthur went up to Trinity Hall, in the autumn of 1881. Both were soon happy in the new life opening up, their paths smoothed by ample allowances. Arthur found plenty of friends. He joined the Amateur Dramatic Club, played football for his college, hacked and hunted from Hopkins' livery stables and, like most of his contemporaries in that age, was not over-troubled by academic requirements. With Douglas Hooper of Trinity Hall, another freshman, he would drive over in a smart high dog cart to Newmarket for the races, and in the evenings there were card parties.

On returning to Cambridge for the start of his second year, in October 1882, Arthur Polhill-Turner was amused to find town and University placarded with posters announcing the forth-coming visit of the American evangelists Moody and Sankey. Polhill-Turner, Hooper and their friends thought it a great joke that two uneducated Americans should be coming to preach to the University. Then every undergraduate received a personal invitation signed by J. E. K. Studd. At Eton Arthur had admired the Studds for their cricket, but had thought them odd to hold Bible readings in their studies. Like most of his social class, he rated the open propagation of religion by such men as the Studds and S. P. Smith, last year's Varsity stroke, as indecent.

The coming of the evangelists was a constant topic of conversation during the first weeks of term. On Guy Fawkes' night, Sunday, 5th November, 1882, Arthur went gaily along to the Corn Exchange where the first meeting was to be held, and joined the large crowd of undergraduates who had come to see the fun. Before the meeting began there was plenty of rowdiness, and he noticed Gerald Lander, a Trinity friend and one of the fast set, happily making a fool of himself piling up chairs in a pyramid. When the platform party of dons and clergymen entered with the evangelists there was clapping and cheering, and a small but noisy section cried 'Encore!' when Sankey sang and 'Hear! Hear!' when Moody prayed. With most of the audience Arthur deplored this as bad sportsmanship. He did his best to listen to the address. A short, thick-set man, was his memory of Moody, 'with a broad American accent and rather a dramatic manner, as he preached on Daniel, representing him as a man dressed in a frock coat, and carrying in his tail pocket a scroll and drawing it out with gusto.' The sermon interested Arthur but did not move him, secure in his destiny as a clergyman.

The meetings for the University moved to the smaller Gymnasium, but by Thursday there were strange rumours. Vast crowds had attended the Town meetings; and Moody was reaching the most unexpected Varsity men. Lander, the rowdy of Sunday night, had been among the first to face the shocked amazement of friends by mounting the iron ladder to the Enquiry Room. Douglas Hooper, a heavy smoker, living only for Newmarket and racing, was already a changed man. Throughout the University the opposition or the amused tolerance of that first Sunday night was giving place to a spirit of the most earnest searching after God. Arthur Polhill-Turner was gripped as Moody preached, as Sankey sang *There were Ninety and Nine* or *Man of Sorrows*. He sensed a 'true tinge of manliness' in Moody. 'The searching address began to penetrate,' he recalled. 'The scathing denunciations of sin at times were terrific, but were always balanced by the wonderful love of God to sinners.' Moody spoke of the Prodigal Son, and pictured the life led by so many of the audience, 'the hollow, drifting life with feeble, mundane ambitions—utterly selfish, giving no service, making no sacrifice, tasting the moment, gliding feebly down the stream of time to the roaring cataract of death'. Arthur began to realize the conceit and emptiness of his existence: his plan to use the sacred ministry to earn an easy livelihood must stink in the nostrils of a holy God. Where would he be going to in Eternity? Yet God loved him, and he died on the Cross that his sins might be washed away. He listened more intently to the 'tender voice that drew us on to trust in a loving Heavenly Father who cared for us. There was pardon for all, a present Saviour'. Memories of Nannie Readshaw floated through his mind. He recalled her telling him that the Lord Jesus wanted to enter his heart. He remembered his rejection of his sister's attempt to bring him and Cecil to Christ, and he knew himself for an ungrateful, selfish cad. 'Just *accept* Him,' Moody was crying, as he came to the end of his address, 'in a moment, in the twinkling of an eye you may be His – nestling in His arms – with the burden of sin and selfishness resting at His feet'.

Arthur Polhill-Turner did not go up the iron ladder. Back in Trinity Hall he faced the cost. He could never accept Christ unless the decision were wholehearted. Half measures were repugnant. Life would have 'to be a good deal readjusted'. If he came out on Christ's side he might meet ridicule and the loss of friends, for though Hooper, Swann and others of his set had become Christians there were plenty who had not. Furthermore since Christ had given all for him, he would have to obey Christ in all things wherever He might Lead; no other way was honest.

As Arthur thought on these things he was afraid.

At the Friday and Saturday meetings he listened again, knowing he must yield yet not daring to do so. On the Sunday 12th November, 1882, the last day of the Mission, the meeting was back in the Corn Exchange. 'A wonderful change from the previous Sunday,' he wrote, 'a crowded gathering, but so still that you might hear a pin drop: a sense of awe and realization of the presence of God.' Moody preached on the message of the Angel in Luke: 'Fear not, for behold I bring you good tidings of great joy, for unto you is born a Saviour.' 'I firmly believe it is the best news that ever came from Heaven to earth,' he began. Arthur sat intent as Moody spoke of the meaning of the Cross and the fact of the Resurrection, and of the enemies which Christ had conquered – death, sin and judgment. And as he listened, he heard a text which struck the scales from his eyes. 'Behold, God is my salvation: I will trust and not be afraid: for the Lord Jehovah is my strength and my song; he also is become my salvation' (Is.7.2).

'I will trust and not be afraid' – his fears were groundless. If Christ had died to save, He lived to keep. There was nothing to fear; the Lord would prove not only a strength but a song.

The words from Isaiah were ringing in his heart as the address continued. 'If you will take my advice,' Moody was saying, 'you will decide the question, and decide this night.' He heard him close with the words, 'Believe the gospel and make room for God in your hearts.' The next moment Arthur was singing in all sincerity the words of the hymn, 'Just as I am, without one plea . . . O Lamb of God, I come.' The hymn ended, all knelt or sat with bowed heads while Moody led in prayer. Then, as the congregation continued in silent prayer, Moody asked all who had received blessing during the week to stand up in token of their faith.

All over the Corn Exchange men stood, some two hundred or more. Among them was Arthur Polhill-Turner.

The Moody mission stirred and renewed many already in the Christian Union. One was William Hoste of Trinity, who had now gone up to Ridley Hall. The evidence of God's love and power in bringing men to Himself had humbled him and set him on fire to serve Christ.

When term ended early in December Hoste returned home to Brighton determined to win his younger brother Dixon, on winter's leave from his battery in the Isle of Wight, a reserved and silent man of twenty-one. The Hostes, a Norfolk family, were descended from a Flemish Protestant who had fled from religious persecution in the 16th century. D. E. Hoste's great-uncle had gone to sea under Nelson and had been made a baronet for brilliant services in the Napoleonic wars; while his grandfather, Sir George, had distinguished himself in the Army. Dixon himself was a good soldier and working hard for eventual promotion.

The children of Major-General and Mrs. Hoste had been brought up, somewhat severely, in the 'fear and nurture of the Lord', but Dixon (Dick to his family) considered the formal religion of the garrison church sufficient for his needs; any further devotion would be detrimental to his professional interests. Willie, however, had seen what God could do at Cambridge and was not disheartened by Dick's lack of interest. Nor did he think it mere chance that Moody and Sankey, fresh from Cambridge and Oxford, were now in Brighton.

Dick refused to attend the Mission, to his mother's distress. On the third or fourth evening, as he sat reading in the drawing room at Havelock Lodge, she came in dressed for the meeting, and again asked him to come with her. He declined, and reluctantly she left him deep in an armchair in front of the fire reading the evening paper. Hardly had the street door banged when, unexpectedly, he heard William get up and come across the room. 'Come on, Dick,' said William in a strangely compelling voice, 'Put on your wraps and go with me to the meeting.' Almost in spite of himself Dick dropped the paper, went down to the hall and put on his ulster, and the two brothers walked to the Dome.

They arrived late, and sat at the back. Dick looked idly at the platform party of clergymen, and listened apathetically to the singing of congregation and choir, led by a portly man with black side-whiskers. A man in ordinary layman's clothes came on the platform. Dick found himself watching with more interest than he had expected.

Then Moody prayed. Hoste was amazed. He had never before heard a man talk to God as a Friend who was present beside him, and yet with utter reverence and humility. The address began, and at once his attention was riveted. 'As Mr. Moody, with intense earnestness and directness,' he recalled in after years, 'preached the solemn truths concerning God's judgment of the impenitent and ungodly, and seriously warned his hearers to flee from the wrath to come, a deep sense of my sinful and perilous state laid hold of my soul with great power.' The facade of pride and indifference crumbled. He realized how dissatisfied he had been for months past. He remembered how he had felt when a woman on the promenade chanced to give him a tract. He knew how much he envied Willie's evident happiness.

God was calling him to repent and give his life to Christ. He had heard the message a hundred times, but the time of rejection was over. Yet he could not accept a break with the easy-going habits of the world, or ridicule,or the possible effect on his career.

The next fortnight was agony. Indifference and hostility had disappeared, but Dick could not bring himself to meet the cost of the decision which must be made. He went repeatedly to the Moody meetings, but confided little in his mother and brother. William, conscious of the struggle but unaware of God's larger plan, of which D. E. Hoste's conversion would be only a part, prayed determinedly.

On the last night of the Mission, General and Mrs. Hoste and William went early to the Dome. Dick slipped in to the back of the hall, miserable in his unresolved conflict. During the hymns and Sankey's solos his depression was acute. Moody began to speak, and in Hoste's mind a sense of the sinfulness of his pettily selfish life grew until it was overwhelming. Moreover he became convinced that 'now is the accepted time, now is the time of salvation', that if he prevaricated further he was lost. He knew that his need, here and in Eternity, outweighed the cost of the decision. He knew Christ had died to bear his sin, and that simple trust alone was necessary. When Moody's address was over and the whole congregation knelt in prayer, Hoste took his heart in his hands, threw doubts aside and gave himself, a guilty sinner, unreservedly to Christ.

To his amazement an immediate sense of peace and content flooded his mind. Not only was Hoste conscious of instant forgiveness but of the unfathomable graciousness of the God whom he had resisted; fears for the future were swallowed up in realization that it could hold nothing better than to know and adore and serve this glorious Lord of life and joy. Only a few moments had passed, yet the old existence seemed an age away.

Moody had finished praying, and called for all those who had received Christ that night, or wished to do so, to come forward. Men and women began to leave their places. And William, sitting in the centre of the hall with his parents and sisters, saw with surprise which turned at once into thanksgiving the soldierly figure of his brother, with a look on his face which showed he no longer sought but had found, going up the aisle in open confession of faith.

In Bedfordshire that winter of 1882-3 another young subaltern was given a shock by his brother.

Cecil Polhill-Turner had returned to Howbury Hall for his first winter's leave after joining the Queen's Bays in Ireland, and was enjoying the hunting and shooting. When Arthur came down from Cambridge Cecil noticed that he seemed in remarkably good form. On the Sunday they were walking across the park to the parish church at Renhold. Cecil made some casual remark about Arthur's succession to the family living, and received the surprise of his life; Arthur replied that he probably would not take the living but 'thought of going to preach in China'. Cecil was horrified, as he knew would be their mother. 'Of course I could not see the slightest object in such a wild scheme,' he recalled, 'and endeavoured to dissuade him.'

Arthur had never looked back from that Sunday evening, 12th November, 1882, when he had given his life to Christ. Determined to do nothing half-heartedly he and Douglas Hooper had made a clean break from the old life of theatres, dancing, racing and cards. 'One's mind was set on grander, deeper themes,' was Arthur's comment, and they regarded academic work and sport principally as a means of witnessing to their new-found faith. Kynaston Studd, Montague Beauchamp and others of the Christian Union became their firm friends. They crowded into the Daily Prayer Meeting, and discovered a particular niche for Trinity Hall in evangelistic and social work in the slum parish of St. Matthew's. Thus the last half of term was in marked contrast to the first.

Several of them, in their willingness to make any response for which Christ called, became aware of an impelling sense of responsibility to proclaim the gospel overseas, though Moody himself had said little or nothing about this. Hooper's mind was directed towards Africa, Tyndale Biscoe towards

India, and Polhill-Turner, perhaps through his friendship with Beauchamp, towards China. Thus, of all the Cambridge Seven, Arthur Polhill-Turner was the first to receive an indication that he was bound for China. With a year and a half more at Cambridge, and theological training to follow, his hopes were distant, yet he saw no reason to hide them from Cecil or to shrink from broaching Cecil's own spiritual need.

The conversation on the way to church was followed by serious and disconcertingly personal discussion. Cecil had plenty of cogent arguments to counter those of Arthur. Arthur, however, was not dismayed. Alice was praying, and Nannie Readshaw in her retirement, to whom Arthur had written the news of his conversion, and old Mrs. Symons at Ravensden, though as yet he had not met her. Arthur seemed to get nowhere. 'But,' wrote Cecil afterwards, 'all the time I knew he was right.'

By the time Cecil returned to his regiment, which shortly moved to Aldershot, Arthur had extracted from him a promise to read a verse or two from the Bible every morning. 'And this I conscientiously did,' wrote Cecil, 'though often it was rather irksome, adding a brief collect as a prayer.'

Cecil was an honest man, if slow in thought. He did not despise or ignore Arthur's faith, but he was determined not to follow until certain the ground. Twice he went with Arthur to Moody's meetings in London and was impressed. He read the *Memorials of Captain Hedley Vicars*, a best-selling biography of a courageous and earnest, though rather introspective, officer killed in the Crimean War. Cecil, on reading it, 'thought it was too sad a business to be a Christian, and always thinking of your sins'. In time he understood better the true meaning of Christian faith; already, however, he realized that coming out for Christ would put an end to easy-going habits and involve possible isolation from his friends in the Mess, even a measure of ridicule and persecution, for high spirited cavalry subalterns had no liking for a man whose faith made him different. And Cecil knew he could never be a worldly or secret Christian; it must be outright, unashamed faith or nothing. Furthermore, he saw that yielding to Christ would involve submission to His will. 'You will have to do what God tells you,' he told himself, 'and He might send you off in another direction.' 'I was very fond of my profession,' commented Cecil, 'wanted to succeed in it, and had plans in my mind; what if all of them should be overturned? At this I hesitated long.'

Thus throughout the summer and autumn of 1883, during the routine of cavalry life at Aldershot, drill and riding school, exercises in the Long Valley, polo and cricket, and card evenings in the mess, Cecil Polhill-Turner was conscious that 'the Holy Spirit was quietly at work, putting thoughts into my mind'.

For his winter's leave Cecil decided to go to Stuttgart, where his uncle, Sir Henry Barron, was British Resident at the court of the Kingdom of Wurtemburg. Cecil took lodgings with a German family to study the language, and his uncle, a wealthy bachelor who had named Cecil as his heir, saw to it that he had a good time. 'Little did he know what was passing in my mind as together we went to the opera, and took long drives; but daily I pondered the Scriptures and thought, yes and prayed.' The call of Christ grew more insistent, objections seemed to be answered one by one. As the weeks drew on, the quiet internal argument continued, until the time came to leave Germany.

There was no violent emotion, no outward sign of a struggle which had lasted over a year, but 'when at last all goodbyes were said, and I stepped into the railway carriage on my return to Aldershot, it was with a mind fully made up. I had yielded to and trusted in Jesus Christ as my Saviour, Lord and Master'.

Chapter 4

THE MAN OF PRAYER

Far away in China a man was riding slowly through the crowded streets of Taiyuan, capital of the province of Shansi in northern China, four hundred miles inland from the sea. As his pony threaded its way among the coolies and beggars and merchants, or stood aside for a mandarin's chair to pass, the rider would now and again acknowledge greetings from passers-by or smile patiently at the scowls of the ill-disposed. He wore a plain Chinese gown and cap, with his hair done in the customary pigtail, and only a second glance showed him to be a westerner – Harold Schofield, a brilliant young Oxford doctor who had sacrificed his prospects and immured himself in China for the sake of Christ.

Schofield dismounted at the door of the unimpressive house of the China Inland Mission and went inside. After a quick look at the dispensary, lest urgent cases had come while he had been out in the villages, he went across to the living room and greeted his wife. A meal was ready but he declined it, and after a few moments' talk Schofield climbed the rickety stairs to the bedroom.

For a few moments he looked out on to the street, crowded, noisy, and with that constant stench of dung and offal, of unwashed bodies and the mingling smells of the shops and houses. As his eye

45

travelled down the street towards the river, and then across to the distant hills, he thought once again of the teeming life of the city and province – nine million Christless inhabitants, and only five or six missionaries among them. He thought of the peasants, toiling in the wheat and rice fields, of the aristocratic mandarins in their palaces and estates, of the women and their cramped, cheerless lives, of the countless temples, and gods of plaster, stone or wood. And then his mind turned to home, so far away – twenty days to the coast, six weeks by sea and land to England. The Church in Britain cared little for these millions in the vast Chinese Empire, slowly waking from the sleep of ages. Few enough were ready to leave comfort and security to bring them the gospel. And of those who had come, and had penetrated inland, scarcely one was a university man, trained in mind and body for leadership. Yet Schofield, a prizeman of Manchester, London and Oxford, knew from his own experience how greatly such men were needed.

The names Polhill-Turner, Hoste, Beauchamp or S. P. Smith meant nothing to him, but once again, this Spring evening of 1883, Harold Schofield knelt at the bedside and unburdened himself in prayer. He prayed that God would waken the Church to China's claims, that He would raise up men to preach His word. Above all that He would touch the universities and call men of talent and ability and consecrate them to His work in China. It seemed a prayer absurd enough except to faith. When Schofield had left England two and a half years earlier at the age of twenty-nine missionary recruits from the universities had been scarce.

Africa and India drew such as there were. His own mission was young and obscure. But the burden was on him; again and again in the past weeks he had found himself drawn aside to pray, leaving food and leisure for prayer to a God who answered prayer.

As the daylight faded in the little bedroom, Schofield was still on his knees, pouring out his soul for that which he would never live to see.

Back in England, unaware of a man's prayers in China, D. E. Hoste the gunner subaltern had been amazed at the immediate sequel to his decision in the Dome at Brighton – his doubts and lack of interest swept away, his moodiness replaced by an almost ecstatic sense of the presence and joy of Christ, the Bible transformed from a dreary compilation to a revelation which it was a privilege and delight to study.

Within a fortnight or less he was beginning to feel the urge to devote his life to the gospel. Nothing else seemed worthy. 'It has changed my life, I want to make it known where Christ is not known. There are many people in other lands who have never heard it, and the Lord wants them to hear it, for He says so. *I want to give my life to this.*' He took his determination to his father, whom he knew was thoroughly sympathetic, and asked permission to resign his commission and go abroad as a missionary. To his disappointment, General Hoste refused. He pointed out how recent was Dick's faith, and reminded him that, though nothing could break its reality, the intensity of his emotions might be transient. To rush, on impulse, to such a binding decision would be foolishly wrong and might afterwards be regretted.

Thus rebuked, D. E. Hoste returned at the end of his leave to the battery Fort at Sandown in the Isle of Wight. His first step was to inform his Battery Commander, an irascible, fault-finding man, of his decision for Christ. The news was received more calmly than Hoste had expected, and his brother-officers took the matter without undue excitement or disgust. Hoste continued his work with ability but his heart was elsewhere' 'One could not but be struck by his most earnest conviction,' recalled a young officer in the battery. 'My recollection is that he was on fire with it all, and that he never really thought of anything else. He spent all his spare time studying the Bible, and in teaching and preaching on the beach and elsewhere.'

Hoste's thoughts went repeatedly to the Mission Field. He was in constant correspondence with William, back at Ridley Hall, and heard of the rising tide of missionary enthusiasm in Cambridge. One day in the spring of 1883 William sent some literature of the China Inland Mission, probably given him by Beauchamp. The China Inland Mission was little known to the world and had been established only eighteen years. Its principles and practice seemed a challenge and an encouragement to the Cambridge men, and to D. .E. Hoste: 'I became deeply impressed,' he wrote, 'by the single-hearted, self-denying devotaion to the cause of the gospel in China which characterized the writing of Mr. Hudson Taylor and others. The lines of simple and direct faith in God for temporal supply and protection . . . the close identification of the missionaries with the Chinese . . . the combination of firm and clear grasp of fundamental truth with a wide and tolerant spirit in regard to ecclesiastical distinction . . . drew out my sympathy.'

Above all he was moved intensely by Hudson Taylor's booklet, *China's Spiritual Need and Claims*, with its devastating revelation of three hundred and eighty-five millions in China 'utterly and hopelessly beyond the reach of the gospel', and its clear call to 'think of the imperative command of our great Captain and Leader, "Go ye into all the world, and preach the gospel to every creature" '. As D. E. Hoste read Hudson Taylor's quietly insistent demand, 'Can the Christians of England sit still with folded arms while these multitudes are perishing?', he could not ignore it, and 'the overwhelming spiritual need of the Chinese began to burden my heart'.[1]

As if to strengthen his growing consciousness that this call was of God, he received in May a letter from his father giving him leave to resign his commission if he still wished to go abroad. During the next two months his burden for the Chinese increased. Hudson Taylor had lately returned from China. Hoste decided to see him but nervously sent William to prepare the way. Then, on 23rd July 1883, utterly unconscious that he was making the first move in an event which should strike the world, D. E. Hoste wrote in his rather boyish hand

1. For Hudson Taylor's extraordinary story see the present writer's *Hudson Taylor and Maria*, or the six volume study by A. J. Broomhall, *Hudson Taylor and China's Open Century*.

to Hudson Taylor: 'Sir; I have for some time been thinking about offering myself for the China Inland Mission. . . '.

This was the season of drills and inspections and Hoste could not get leave until the first week of August. Interviewed in the small house in Mildmay, North London, which served as the C. I. M. headquarters, Hoste was much struck with the fifty-one-year-old missionary, his kindliness of manner and unobtrusive humour, his steel-hardened will tempered by the indefinable redolence of Christ's presence. But if Hoste, with a half-admitted belief that a gunner subaltern was an important catch, expected to be received with open arms, he was disappointed. As with his father in January, so with Hudson Taylor in August. Hudson Taylor damped Hoste's enthusiasm, stressing the dangers and isolations of work in China, the possibility of repudiation by both Chinese and Westerners, and the severity of the spiritual strain on the most mature. At the end of their conversation, Hoste promised to wait patiently and prayerfully, taking no further action for a while.

Hoste had been humbled again, and realized how clearly he must seek God's will. But before the cab had dropped him at Victoria Station for his return to Brighton, he was conscious more than ever of the depth of his desire to go to China.

In Shansi, Harold Schofield lay dying of virulent diptheria, caught from a Chinese who had crept in unawares to the mission surgery. His prayers were unceasing until the end, and still concentrated on his passion of the past months, that God would awaken the universities of Britain to China's need.

On 1st August, 1883 a few days before Hudson Taylor interviewed Hoste, Harold Schofield died.

Chapter 5

'I WILL SEND THEE FAR HENCE. . .'

Meanwhile, decisive events were occurring in the life of S. P. Smith. The first, though none realized it, was his acceptance of a holiday tutorship during the summer vacation of 1882 before taking up work at Newlands, his brother-in-law's school in South London. His pupil was George Burroughes, a Winchester boy, the younger brother of Harry Burroughes of Trinity and, as it happened, a cousin of D. E. Hoste. On 9th August Smith arrived at their home at Normanstone, near Lowestoft in Norfolk. 'The happiest five weeks of my life,' was Smith's verdict. Not only was there tennis and sailing and duck-shooting, but the Burroughes were thorough going Christians. Smith took part in cottage meetings, open-air hymn-singing, visiting and a regular work among the navvies building the new Lowestoft docks. Among the many neighbours to whom he was introduced at Normanstone was a Mr. Price, an elderly Christian of delightful character who lived in a small house in Pakefield, a village on the coast a mile or two south of Lowestoft.

In mid-September Smith took up quarters at Newlands School, 'earning my own livelihood , beginning life in earnest'. The work was light and congenial and his athletic prowess and his 'bright, attractive personality' made him popular with the boys. Lloyd Griffith allowed him ample free time, in which he would go to London or Aldershot or Windsor to speak at soldiers' or young men's meetings. His heart was increasingly in Christian service, yet a streak of selfishness showed he had much to learn: more than once the staff of Newlands was knocked up in the small hours to let him in.

In November he was given a long weekend to go up to Cambridge during Moody's mission. Praying with Beauchamp, Kynaston Studd and Hoste, encouraging old rowing friends to hear Moody and talking with one or another afterwards, 'straight to the point' until long past midnight – all this, with a little rowing for old times' sake, and the Mission meetings themselves, gave S. P. one of the best weekends he could remember. The Mission's impact on the University made him almost envious of his friends, who would be able to reap where Moody was sowing. On the final Sunday night he helped in the Enquiry Room 'and spoke to Duthort of Caius, who went away having found *Him*'. 'Afterwards Smith was introduced to 'dear old Moody', through whose preaching seven years earlier he had been converted, and 'gave him such a shake of the hand!'

S. P. Smith returned to Newlands with deepened devotion. His eldest brother Ernest, at Twickenham, found a walk with him the means of restoration to single-minded service. At the school one boy after another would come to his room for 'a talk and a read', often with lasting result. But for all this, S. P. was not satisfied. 'What an eventful year it has been,' he wrote on 31st December, 'perhaps the most eventful year of my life except the year I was by grace enabled to receive Christ. A good deal of very happy service for the Master. . . . How much to cause for thanksgiving! And ever so much cause repentance, shame and sorrow. Oh God, the insincerity, sham and "men service" of the year!'

In this mood he returned to Normanstone for a fortnight's visit to the Burroughes. The first ten days were much as in the summer – driving and walking, battledore and shuttlecock, or word-games in the evening; and Bible readings, hymn singing and evangelistic work among the poor and navvies. On 18th January Mrs. Burroughes and George were to go on ahead to Burlingham Hall, George's grandfather's place some fifteen miles inland, but Harry had wired that he would not be returning that night, and the three unmarried daughters would be left alone except for the servants. Victorian convention demanded that the young bachelor guest must sleep under another roof. Stanley was to lunch with old Mr. Price at Pakefield, and he walked over with a small hand-bag to stay the night as well.

In this trivial manner Smith was led to the second most decisive experience of his life. Price was a man of generosity and spirit – an old people's dinner was proceeding when Stanley arrived, and an evangelistic meeting followed; but he had dis-covered also a secret too little known among Chris-tians in the eighteen-eighties. The Keswick Move-ment was in its infancy. Evan Hopkins' great book, *The Law of Liberty in the Spiritual Life*, was still being written. Handley Moule, soon to be the most scholarly exponent of the movement, was as yet opposing it, while Bishop Ryle of Liverpool, the evangelical leader, opposed it to the last.

But Price of Pakefield had learned (in Evan Hopkins' phrase) 'the secret of liberty and delight in the service of the Lord'. He had proved that on a definite consecration of the whole self to God – not in intent but in simple deed – the Holy Spirit would shed abroad the love of God in the heart, producing a realistic sanctity beyond any previous imagining, and providing a lasting sense of the presence of the Lord, 'turning your life of duty into a life of liberty and love'.

That night of 18th January, 1883, Price and Stanley Smith sat up late. As they talked Smith saw something of the self-will that was hindering him. Because he enjoyed Christian activities he did them, but the direction remained in his hands. There were blemishes in his character; and no 'hourly abiding', in the presence of Christ. Price showed him, as Moule was to show Smith's Cambridge friends the following year, that because God is 'an eternal person undertaking for you' it is possible to 'walk with God all day long, to love God with all our heart and our neighbour as ourselves, to cast every care on Him daily and to be at peace amidst pressure; and . . . by unreserved resort to divine power under divine conditions to become strongest through and through at our weakest point'. Such was true sanctity, making 'not the slightest compromise with the smallest sin', and rejoicing in the Lord. But it could only occur, said Price, when Stanley denied himself and took up the Cross, when he handed himself a willing slave unreservedly dedicated to his Master's service, to the Christ who had died to redeem him and who lives, as the New Testament showed, to 'keep you from falling and present you faultless before the presence of his glory with exceeding joy'.

It was after midnight when they went up to their rooms. Stanley Smith had never before seen so vividly the meaning of God's holiness and of his own sin, nor the demands and the possibilities of faith in Christ. Before he got into bed he sat down and wrote in his diary, 'I must *fully* consecrate myself'.

The next morning they talked again and read Bible passages. Stanley understood from Romans 7 and 2 Corinthians vii and Ephesians 5 that it was to Christians, and therefore to such as himself, that the commands were given, 'Present your bodies a living sacrifice, holy, acceptable unto God', 'Let us cleanse ourselves from all filthiness of the flesh and spirit, perfecting holiness in the fear of God', and, 'Be filled with the Spirit'. When they read in St. John and Acts he longed to appropriate the promises of Christ to His apostles, 'My peace I give unto you. . . . Ask and ye shall receive, that your joy may be full. . . . Ye shall receive power after that the Holy Ghost is come upon you.' And the secret lay in accepting the challenge of the night before, to consecrate himself fully. Since his decision three years earlier, with Waldegrave at Cambridge, 'by God's grace to live for and to Him', Smith had learned to know himself better and to know Christ better, and thus re-consecration must be on a deeper, more costly level.

Christ was calling, and Smith was in no mind for

refusal. Before morning was out he knelt down with Price in the little room in the East Coast village, and prayed that the Lord would take his whole life to use it as He wished.

At midday he left Price and walked back to Lowestoft for his navvies' meeting. As he went, 'very happy', he found himself singing 'My all is on the altar'. At the meeting he experienced a new freedom in speaking. The navvies filled the cramped hall, late-comers content to remain outside in the raw January inshore wind. 'His word was with power not mine,' wrote Smith. 'These dear men with their grasp of the hand and "God bless you, sir!" repay anything.' He arrived back at Normanstone to find lunch almost over, but the Burroughes girls 'very kindly stayed while I talked a little about Him, for my heart was so full'. After lunch they all went to the drawing room and Stanley opened his Bible, which seemed to speak with a new and 'most delightful' voice.

In the evening, he took the train inland to Burlingham, not to stay with the Burroughes at the Hall but with their neighbours the Jarys at Burlingham House. This brief visit clinched his new experience. Jary was 'very helpful', and showed him the verse from Malachi, 'Bring ye all the tithes into the storehouse. . . and prove me now herewith, saith the Lord of hosts, if I will not open you the windows of heaven, and pour you out a blessing, that there shall not be room enough to receive it'. The next day, 'very happy in the Lord', Stanley Smith walked across to the Hall. Only Harry was in, and Smith told him that he had 'laid all on the altar'. In the afternoon he visited a bedridden cottager. She, too, had learned the secret; she gave him her motto, 'In all things He might have the pre-eminence'; and 'she took me to heaven's gate'.

The last full day of his visit, Sunday, 21st January, was a 'most lovely bright sunshiny day and my soul felt like the weather'. Walking to church he was able to give decided help to a fellow guest, a backslider. Twice during the day he was asked to speak at local meetings and was conscious that 'the Spirit hit them hard'. Travelling to London on the Monday he talked to three different strangers about their souls and felt it well worth while. And as soon as he was home in John Street he was telling his sister 'of the blessing I have got'.

Smith's experience at Lowestoft was revolutionary, and lasting. 'Bless the dear Lord, He is in me and *fills* me,' he was writing a week later, back at Newlands, 'How good He is. Oh that all Christians knew this full surrender!' 'Christ is my life! How sweet it is,' '''Singing all the while,'' this is heaven,' 'Everlasting joy,' such were his feelings in the first weeks. In due course ecstasy settled to an abiding contentment, but the burning fire of his love did not decrease. At every opportunity he 'let out about my blessing', not to vaunt his spirituality but because, like the apostles, he could 'not but speak' of the things which he had heard and seen. The only compulsion was the overwhelming sense of God's goodness, the joy of Christ's presence and the knowledge that He offered a like experience to all.

At Newlands he delighted to show the boys who worked or played games with him *The Light of the World*, hanging in his room, and the text beneath,

Revelation 3.20, 'my favourite verse': 'Behold I stand at the door and knock; if any man hear my voice and open the door, I will come in.' In London he was constantly at evangelistic or holiness meetings. Despite his blessing he knew there was more to come, and at a meeting of Wilson Carlile's recently formed Church Army he did not scruple to go up to the penitent form to pray for 'the baptism of the Holy Ghost for service and to be made *whole*'.

The new wine was of such potency that occasional extravagancies were almost inevitable. At Hitchen during the Easter holidays, taking part in an Open Air in the Market Place, he and some friends 'went down on our knees and agonized to the dear Lord for souls'. On the way home he found himself alone in a railway carriage with three well-dressed young men, 'probably Varsity'. When he 'spoke to them definitely about their souls, they thought me mad and pooh-poohed. So after very straight talking I knelt down and prayed,' and for the rest of the way to King's Cross the three young men sheltered uncomfortably behind their newspapers while S. P. Smith knelt on the dusty floor of the Great Northern compartment and prayed aloud!

Whether always wise, nothing could suppress Smith's zeal, or detract from the sterling courage with which he set about his witness to faith and holiness, and his God-given task of bringing souls to Christ. With Algernon Dudley Ryder, who had succeeded E. W. Moore at the Brunswick Chapel, and E. J. Kennedy of the Y. M. C. A., Smith would go out to Hyde Park on Sundays for Open Airs beside the Reformers' Tree near Marble Arch, where the roughs congregated in their scores. In mid-June, courageously, they held their first Open Air near Hyde Park Corner, where the fashionable world would saunter after church. It was a striking scene, the three smartly dressed young men – Ryder was only thirty-five – standing by the Achilles Statue, their silk hats laid beside them, while Smith's voice rang out across strolling knots of fine ladies with their bustles and flowered hats, and gentlemen in tight frock coats with gay button-holes. 'We began by singing a hymn, and after being "eyed" well up and down, I began to speak. Then Ryder very faithfully on "Come out". Then Kennedy. The Lord managed everything. . . . One lady was deeply touched and gave her name and address, and another gentleman felt stirred as being a Christian who hid his profession.' After that , Ryder and Smith were often out. At twenty-three Smith was now an 'athletic, handsome man of winning address and manners', and his courageous stand impressed his contemporaries. 'Smith could *hold* the Sunday Parade throng,' wrote one friend, and that was no mean feat. 'The Lord was there with power,' was his own comment, and on one occasion, at Stanhope Gate, several were weeping before he had done.

Smith was no ranter. He spoke forcibly, if some-times too long and a little verbose, and his words came from the heart, backed by a wealth of Scrip-tural allusion and clear in their aim. He was much in demand for meetings and, his old ill-health for-gotten, he travelled long distances with apparently inexhaustible energy. In personal talks he was used even more. To Christians he stressed 'definite consecration', to others their need of a personal Saviour, while his theme was always 'an all-sufficient Christ'. He resolved that 'God helping me I will never miss another opportunity of speaking definitely to a man about his soul when he is alone with me', and since corridor trains did not exist on Victorian railways he had ample opportunity to fulfil his vow.

Behind it all was the study of the Word, and prayer. Smith knew that the mere telling a man about Christ was not enough, that a spiritual conflict was involved which could only be won by prayer. Sometimes he would spend his spare time at Newlands entirely in prayer and Bible reading. Whenever he could he would preface a public address by a long period of prayer in private, and as he prayed he learned to lay hold more surely on the promises of God, and to see His extensive response.

No sacrifice now seemed too great, not for its own sake, as three years earlier, but for the sake of extending Christ's kingdom. He sold his furniture, content to exist with the comfortless minimum which the school provided, and gave the money 'to the Lord's work'. Smith was not a fanatic. He knew that neither mind nor body nor spirit could be kept on the stretch without pause, and was not above relaxing in a game of fives or tennis, but the world seemed trivial and transitory. He was impatient of its customs and conventions, and thought nothing of giving his best clothes away to a tramp or walking long distances to save a few pennies on an omnibus journey. His passion was for Christ, and for the souls of men.

Eighteen eighty-three wore on. For all his activity S. P. Smith was still unaware of his life's work. He wondered whether to join Wilson Carlile in the Church Army, relieving the miseries of the poor; or to stay at Newlands, for although his heart was no longer in teaching the opportunities were great. He was certain that ordination in the Church of England would seem restricting, and as for the Foreign Mission field, he believed himself still bound by the command he had been given in October 1880 through Ezekiel iii. 5, 'Thou art not sent to a people of a strange speech'. He could not forget the Christless millions abroad, but until he received clear guidance to the contrary he could not disobey the command.

He was constant in prayer for clear direction but throughout the autumn no answer was given. Early in November he was invited by Handley Moule, a sure tribute, to address the men of Ridley Hall and their friends on the subject of Holiness. Monty Beauchamp, now a Ridley theological student, was there, and Smith met Arthur Polhill-Turner for the first time.

At the end of the month Smith had five days' leave from the school. He went to London and spoke at a Y. M. C. A. The next day he lunched with Monty Beauchamp in Cromwell Road and they went together to Wandsworth to hear Moody, who had started his Second London Campaign which, by using a portable hall, the original 'tin tabernacle', was centring successively on four strategic areas. The day ended with an address by Smith at Lord Radstock's Mission at Mortlake. The following afternoon, 29th November, Smith set off to fulfil a long-standing engagement at a small convention at Brockham near Dorking. He missed his train at Charing Cross and only reached his hosts a few minutes before he was due to speak.

The next day came the guidance for which he had prayed. The detail is missing, for the relevant diary pages were lost during Smith's subsequent travels but the fact is clear:'On November 30th 1883 I got set free from Ezekiel iii. 5 by the Lord giving me Isaiah 6: "I will also give thee for a light to the Gentiles, that thou mayest be my salvation unto the end of the earth" '.

Stanley Smith was in no doubt. It was a call to foreign service. God was sending him 'far hence to the Gentiles'.

Smith's prayers and interest had long followed the China Inland Mission. Its uncompromising spirituality and its tolerance attracted him as they attracted Hoste and it carried the gospel 'not where Christ was named'. Before the end of the year Stanley Smith had written to the C. I. M. and on 4th January, 1884, he went down in the morning to Mildmay, though suffering from gastric trouble, 'to call on Mr. Hudson Taylor of the China Inland Mission. Stayed till 8 p.m. Had tea there and a nice long talk about *China*; I hope to labour for God there soon.' The 'very bad attack of sickness' during the subsequent night at John Street did not blight his memory of the interview, for he knew now that China was his destined place of service.

Early in the new term Smith took part in a mission at Clapham, not far from Newlands and in the parish of South Lambeth, where W. W. Cassels was curate. For two years Cassels had worked quietly and selflessly for the crowded slums of South Lambeth. He had already sensed a vocation for overseas service; he had been born in Portugal and had lived there his first ten years until the death of his father, a merchant. But it was not to Europe he expected to go but far afield with the Church Missionary Society. Smith and Cassels had not seen much of each other since Cambridge but the Clapham Mission drew them close. 'After the meetings,' wrote Smith years later, 'we had some arm-in-arm walks and heart-to-heart talks about the Lord and China,' and in those bleak February days Cassels found his missionary interest slowly focusing on inland China.

Stanley Smith's own climax came on Wednesday, 26th March, 'perhaps one of the most important days of my life'. After morning school at Newlands he went up to London and took his mother to the Moody and Sankey meeting, then on a site in Kensington near Olympia. They went on to tea with Moody at the house where he was staying and Moody, who had heard much of Smith's ability and single-mindedness and had seen him at work in the Campaign Enquiry Room, invited him to come over to Massachusetts to help for a while at the missionary training home. That night Hudson Taylor and Algernon Ryder came to dinner at John Street. The whole question of Stanley's missionary call was discussed, Mr. and Mrs. Smith being well prepared to entrust Stanley to the C. I. M. whatever the cost in separation. Hudson Taylor took family prayers and the young candidate, just twenty-four, and the veteran of fifty-two walked together part of Taylor's way home. That night the decision was made: 'Decided to go to China with Hudson Taylor as a missionary,' recorded Smith, 'and to go, D. V., via America so as to see Moody's training home.'

Six days later, on 1st April, Smith was interviewed by a Council Meeting of the C. I. M. and accepted as a probationer.

Hudson Taylor and the C. I. M. Council were still unaware of the larger plan unfolding. A year earlier the Mission had asked the Christian world to pray for seventy 'more labourers. . . called and sent out by God to assist us', but they knew nothing as yet of a Seven. D. E. Hoste had again been interviewed in February 1884 but his unwillingness to rush in where he longed to tread made him hesitant. 'Interview somewhat informal,' ran the Council minutes, 'as Mr. Hoste not quite clear as to his future, but hoping that ultimately he might be able to work in China.' Not until May did Hoste resign his commission in the Gunners, though spending all the time he could with the Moody and Sankey Campaign.

The Council now knew that Schofield had died, and that he had died praying for the universities. After interviewing Stanley Smith on 1st April they found themselves led towards the future by their decision that Smith should hold a number of farewell meetings and remain in England until October, 'so as to have a chance of visiting the Varsities'. The American plan was tacitly dropped.

Down in South Lambeth, as the hot spring and summer of 1884 advanced, Cassels was continuing to feel his way towards China. On 28th July Stanley Smith came for a day for some open-air work in the parish. Smith had spent his spare time during the summer term as before, and at a mission in Aldershot he had met 'Polhill-Turner of the Bays', who gave him warm support. At Lambeth Smith went out with Cassels and some others 'and sung on the streets and then addressed different groups. They seemed very much impressed. Afterwards we swept into a room, and I trust some 9 or 10 decided for Christ.'

When parishioners and converts had gone, Cassels and Smith settled down for a talk. They unburdened their hearts to each other and near midnight walked back together towards Newlands as far as Clapham Common. 'He is much interested in China,' wrote Smith afterwards, 'may the Lord send him out with me!

The Newlands term, Smith's last, ended two days later and Smith went down to Cowes Week as the guest of the Marquess of Ailsa on his yacht *Titannia* – 'In the evening had a very nice service. I spoke on Luke 11. 21. I trust the 2nd Engineer came to the Lord. It is a glorious witness for the Lord, Lord Ailsa who is so well known at Cowes having these services.' Cassels remained in the dust and grime of a South Lambeth August. Both were praying. On 17th August, back in London, Smith went down to South Lambeth. After lunch the two went round to the parish church for 'an hour's blessed waiting on the Lord'. That night Smith wrote of Cassels, 'I trust he now sees his way definitely to go out to China'.

Shortly afterwards, having been informed by the Church Missionary Society, whose Chinese stations were in the Treaty Ports, that they were unable as yet to consider operating inland, Cassels wrote to Hudson Taylor.

On 19th September, 1884, at a C. I. M. function in Aldersgate Street, S. P. Smith, Cassels and D. E. Hoste were together. Hoste and Smith's previous meeting had been the brief encounter in William Hoste's Cambridge rooms in 1880. 'He was *then* in the Artillery,' commented Smith, 'he is now, D. V.' going out to China.' Hoste's acceptance was not yet confirmed, though reasonably certain. Cassel's position was more insecure. His mother, a woman of sincere faith with a strong missionary interest, could not bear the thought of losing William, the only one of her seven sons still in England. In distress she called on Hudson Taylor in Pyrland Road to implore him not to take William. Hudson Taylor, recognizing that this was no worldly opposition, assured her that he held a parent's wishes sacred and would not encourage William if she opposed his response to the call. In the closing days of September Cassels and Hudson Taylor were much in prayer, and on 1st October their reward came in a letter from Mrs. Cassels: 'It is so evident,' she wrote to Hudson Taylor, 'that he sees it to be his duty and his privilege to enter upon the Chinese Mission work, that I should only take the part of a bad Mother to one of the best of sons if I continued to put thorns in his sufficiently difficult road. . . so I must follow, for I could not have led to the course he feels he is led to, and I will try and claim God's gracious promises for him, and for all your work at large.'

Smith's farewell tour had already begun. With

Hudson Taylor he visited Salisbury, Glasgow, Edinburgh and Dublin, returning to London on 16th October, a humbling and sobering experience 'to be with that dear man of God'. The visits to Oxford and Cambridge were to follow and the three young men could then depart quietly in December for their life's work.

But Schofield's prayers were not yet fully answered. The departure was not to be quiet. For a spiritual conflict in the heart and mind of the most brilliant cricketer of the day was about to be resolved, with incalculable results for Smith, his friends and the world.

Chapter 6

TEST CRICKETER

C. T. Studd was bred in luxury. His father, Edward Studd, had returned from jute planting at Tirhoor in North India to spend his fortune. At Hallerton in Leicestershire and later at Tedworth House near Andover the young Studds grew up in a spacious world dedicated to hunting, cricket and their father's fine string of racehorses.

In 1875, when Charlie and his two elder brothers, Kynaston and George, were at Eton their father's sudden conversion through Moody and Sankey made a startling difference to their lives. Edward Studd now thought only of bringing his friends and family to Christ; as his coachman remarked, 'though there's the same skin, there's a new man inside'.

The boys had been brought up in the arid formality of conventional religion, 'a Sunday thing', so C. T. said later, 'like one's Sunday clothes, to be put away on Monday morning'. But now his father was 'a real live play-the-game Christian'. 'But it did make one's hair stand on end,' was C. T.'s memory, telling the story long afterwards to young people, in the merry way he loved to use. 'Everyone in the house had a dog's life of it until they were converted. I was not altogether pleased with him. He used to come into my room at night and ask if I was converted. After a time I used to sham sleep when I saw the door open, and in the day I crept round the other side of the house when I saw him coming.'

The following year Edward Studd's prayers were answered. One by one on a single summer's day at Tedworth Hall, each of his three elder sons, J..E. K., G. B., and C.T., all in the Eton eleven, were won for Christ by a guest, a young man called Weatherby, who had earned their respect by his reaction to a crual practical joke. 'Right then and there joy and peace came into my soul,' recalled C. T., 'I knew then what it is to be "born again", and the Bible, which had been so dry to me before, became everything.'

None of the brothers had courage to tell each other what had happened; it was only disclosed by a joint letter from their father early in the following half at Eton. Edward Studd died shortly afterwards but Kynaston maintained his tradition, organizing a college Bible Reading. Of C. T. , when he left in '79, his housemaster wrote, 'he has done no little good to all who come under his influence'. Sport, however, increasingly absorbed his attention. By determination and hard training rather than by native genius he made himself an outstanding all-rounder and was 'incomparably the best cricketer' in the Eton and Harrow of 1879, when Captain. He was in the racquets pair, and won the House Fives.

Going up to Trinity in 1879, a freshman with Smith, Beauchamp and William Hoste, Studd won his blue and thus played for Cambridge for four consecutive years, following his brother G. B. as Captain in 1883, to be followed by J. E. K. in '84. His national fame dated from his great century in

1882 when Cambridge University, against all expectation, defeated the unbeaten Australians. That August, still an undergraduate, twenty-one years old, he played at the Oval in the famous Test Match which England seemed about to win, yet lost to the Australians by 8 runs, and the term 'The Ashes' was coined. By his Captain's error of judgement in changing the batting order, Studd went in last and never received a ball. The match was so exciting that one spectator gnawed right through the handle of his umbrella.

That year of 1882 C. T. Studd had the highest batting average, and in bowling, though only fifteenth in the averages, had the second highest score of wickets taken. The great W. G. Grace, the Gloucestershire doctor who was the best and most famous cricketer of the Victorian age, described C. T. Studd as 'The most brilliant member of a well-known cricketing family, and from 1881 to 1884 had few superiors as an all-round player. His batting and bowling were very good. . . . His style of batting was free and correct, and he scored largely and rapidly against the best bowlers of his time. He bowled medium-pace, round arm, with a machine-like delivery, and had a fair break from the off.'

By 1883 C. G. Studd was a household name, the idol of undergraduates and schoolboys and the admiration of their elders. But as a Christian he was a nonentity. 'Instead of going and telling others of the love of Christ I was selfish and kept the knowledge all to myself. The result was that gradually my love began to grow cold, the love of the world came in.' Looking back afterwards he felt he had spent these Cambridge years in one long, 'unhappy backsliding state'. In fact, he had not been averse to singing 'Sankeys' round the piano, or to having a 'read and prayer'; he went occasionally to the Daily Prayer Meeting and, as S. P. Smith found, he was willing to take C. I. C. C. U. cards to freshmen. Moreover he was recognized as a Christian, and since cricketing prowess, high spirits, good looks and a kind heart made him outstandingly popular in the University, his identification with the Christian set was not worthless. But he never led another to Christ. Whereas, as he once wrote to Kynaston, 'Our cricketing friends used to call you "The Austere Man" because your life was true to God and you were true to them, for you were ever faithful in speaking to them about their souls', C. T. preferred the easier path. He admired his brother's 'courage and loyalty in the Lord Jesus Christ', and was kept by J. E. K's influence from utter betrayal of his convictions, but his religion was effete: 'mincing, lisping, bated breath, proper,' he once described it, 'hunting the Bible for hidden truths, but no obedience, no sacrifice.'

During Moody's Cambridge mission in the autumn of 1882, C. T. Studd was in Australia with the M. C. C. team which recovered the Ashes, returning in the spring of 1883. By then, S. P. Smith had passed through his great experience of consecration near Lowestoft. Two old ladies, who had known Edward Studd, had set themselves to pray that C. T. be brought to re-dedication, but their prayers seemed unanswered. At the end of the 1883 season C. T. was 'for the second year in succession accorded the premier position as an all-round cricketer. Some years have elapsed,' continued *Wisden's*, 'since the post has been filled by a player so excellent in all three departments of the game.' He was at the very height of cricketing fame.

At the end of November 1883, when S. P. Smith was at Brockham in Surrey receiving definite guidance to the Mission Field, C. T.'s brother George, closest to him in age and affection, fell seriously ill. C. T. came down from Cambridge in December to find G. B.'s life in danger. He was prostrate with grief and anxiety, and as he sat in the sick-room overlooking the street and narrow gardens, while carts and carriages rolled softly by over the straw specially laid down, he began to see life in its true perspective. At night-time, as he waited in the semi-darkness lest his brother should call, he 'saw what the world was worth'. 'As night after night I watched by the bedside as he was hovering between life and death God showed me what the honour, what the pleasure, what the riches of this world were worth. All these things had become as nothing to my brother. He only cared about the Bible and the Lord Jesus Christ, and God taught me the same lesson.'

In the first days of January 1884, Studd could say later, 'God brought me back'. Very humbly he re-consecrated himself to his Lord; and as if to underline that God's hand is in all the accidents of life, 'in His love and goodness He restored my brother to health'. As soon as George was out of danger, C. T. went to Moody's meeting at St. Pancras. 'There the Lord met me again and restored to me the joy of my salvation.'

Immediately, 'and what was better than all',

Studd learned the intense satisfaction of spiritual work. He begun to tell his friends of his decision, taking them to Moody or to evangelistic services in Cambridge, devoting himself to Christ with the same determination which he had devoted to cricket. 'The Lord was very loving and He soon gave me the consolation of saving one of my nearest and dearest friends. I cannot tell you,' he was often to say later, 'what joy it gave me to bring the first soul to the Lord Jesus Christ. I have tasted most of the pleasures that this world can give. I do not suppose there was one that I had not experienced; but I can tell you that those pleasures were as nothing compared to the joy that the saving of that one soul gave me.'

Back in London for the Easter vacation, after his last term in Cambridge, he was constantly helping at the Moody Campaign. S. P. Smith met him there on Sunday, 23rd March, and they walked back together from St. Pancras to Hyde Park Gardens having 'a nice talk'. The cricket season began and C. T. felt he 'must go into the cricket field and get the men there to know the Lord Jesus'. He had found 'something infinitely better than cricket. My heart was no longer in the game; I wanted to win souls for the Lord.' He took members of the Test team to hear Moody. One by one A. J. Webbe, the great batsman, A. G. Steel and Ivo Bligh, the Captain, afterwards Lord Darnley, told Studd that they accepted Christ, and kept in touch with him for the rest of his life.

On 19th June, 1884, the Moody Campaign ended. The combination of cricket and Christian work had kept Studd happy without thought for the future. But now he 'wanted to know what my life's work was to be for the Lord Jesus Christ. I wanted only to serve Him.' Studd was impatient, and conscious of his powers and influence. It was hard not to consider himself an asset to the Christian cause and he expected that he would soon find his niche and make his mark. No clear guidance, however, was granted. He invited the opinion of his friends but they were contradictory. The more he strove to make up his mind the more impatient he became, and within a few weeks of Moody's departure Studd had worked himself into such an emotional tangle that his health gave way and he had to go into the country to convalesce.

During July, August and September, while S. P. Smith, Cassels and Hoste were preparing for China, C. T. Studd was recovering his balance, spending much time in Bible study and in prayer for guidance. His only decision was to read for the Bar 'until the Lord Jesus should show me what my life's work was to be for Him'. As soon as he returned to Hyde Park Gardens early in October even this decision seemed wrong, and he was convinced that he must spend his whole time in Christian service. His inheritance was ample, 'God had given me far more than was sufficient to keep body and soul together. . . . How could I spend the best hours of my life in working for myself and for the honour and pleasures of this world while thousands and thousands of souls are perishing every day without having heard of the Lord Jesus Christ, going down to Christless and hopeless graves?'

Studd's mind worked in single tracks. Whatever

he did must be done to the utter exclusion of other interests'. Awakened as he was, he knew that nothing less than uninhibited dedication to the winning of souls would satisfy him. He 'began to read the Bible more earnestly and to ask God what I was to do. But this time I determined not to consult with flesh and blood, but just wait until God should show me.'

But the first thing God had to show him was himself. Towards the end of September a close friend invited Studd to a drawing-room Bible meeting. A passage was read. As they studied it someone mentioned a woman they all knew. 'Have you heard of the extraordinary blessing Mrs. W. has received? . . . You know she has been an earnest Christian worker for nearly her whole life, and has had a good deal of trouble and sorrow which has naturally weighed upon her. But somehow lately God has given her such a blessing that although she has had so much trial it does not affect her at all now. Nothing seems to trouble her. She lives a life of perfect peace.' They turned to their Bibles again to see whether such a blessing was promised. Before they parted they were convinced that the peace which 'passeth understanding' and 'joy unspeaklable' were offered to every Christian, and they had knelt down to ask that God should 'give us this blessing'.

Back in his own room Studd knelt down again, 'very much in earnest'. Someone had just given him a popular American book, *The Christian's Secret of a Happy Life*. *The Christian's Secret*, by Hannah Pearsall Smith, which was to become a best seller when published in England four years later, dealt in simple, practical terms with the very possibilities which they had been discussing at the Bible meeting. 'In order to enter into this blessed interior life of rest and triumph,' wrote Mrs. Pearsall Smith, 'you have two steps to take – first, entire abandonment, and second, absolute faith.' As Studd read, sometimes on his knees and sometimes sitting in his chair, he began to see that he had not received the blessing because he had been 'keeping back from God what belonged to Him'. 'I had known about Jesus Christ's dying for me, but I had never understood that if he died for me, then I didn't belong to myself. Redemption means "buying back", so that if I belonged to Him, either I had to be a thief and keep what wasn't mine or else I had to give up everything to God. When I came to see that Jesus Christ had died for me, it didn't seem hard to give up all for HIM. It seemed just common, ordinary honesty.'

Convinced that 'I had kept back myself from Him, and had not wholly yielded', C. T. Studd went down on his knees and from the bottom of his heart said the words of Frances Ridley Havergal's hymn

'Take my life and let it be
Consecrated, Lord, to Thee.'

The next step was faith – a straightforward confidence that God had accepted his life because it was offered, and that what He had taken He could keep. Then and there Studd took up the position which was to be his chief characteristic to the day he died: 'I realized that my life was to be one of simple, childlike faith. . . . I was to trust in Him that He would work in me to do His good pleasure. I saw that He was my loving Father and that He would guide me and keep me, and moreover that He was well able to do it.'

What S. P. Smith had discovered near Lowestoft in January 1883, C. T. Studd found in London in September 1884 – peace, security, overflowing contentment and a willingness to go wherever he was sent.

It was not long before light was thrown on the future. Until his recent experience no thought of overseas service had crossed Studd's mind: 'England was big enough for me.' But the call of the foreign field soon became insistent. It was almost a matter of mere mathematics – the percentage of Christless people to every witnessing Christian. Furthermore, the pioneer's blood was stirring in his veins. As for sacrifice, it seemed the wrong word to express the intensity of his joy in being put to God's work.

On Saturday, 1st November, Stanley Smith returned to London from his farewell visits to Cambridge and Oxford. His contacts had been informal – frequent, crowded meetings in the colleges, breakfasts and lunches with twos or threes, brief words at Bible Readings and prayer meetings. At about eleven o'clock in the morning of that Saturday, on his way home from Paddington Station to John Street, Stanley Smith drove up in a hansom cab to Number Two Hyde Park Gardens, to call at the Studds. Both Kynaston and C. T. were in, and when Smith mentioned that he was going that evening to the C. I. M. headquarters to a service of farewell to John McCarthy, a returning missionary, C. T. said he would join him.

At the service McCarthy, one of the founder-members of the C. I. M., told once again the story of his call, nearly twenty years before, and spoke of the vastness of spiritual need in China, 'thousands of souls perishing every day and night without even the knowledge of the Lord Jesus'. As McCarthy spoke, C. T. Studd was convinced that God 'was indeed leading me to China'.

As McCarthy's address closed and they were singing *He leadeth me*, Studd for a moment thought of rising in his place and offering for China on the spot. But he felt 'people would say I was led by impulse'. When the meeting ended he slipped away by himself and prayed for guidance. Only one consideration made him hesitate: he cared not at all that to bury himself in China would end his cricket and snuff out his national reputation, that it might invite the disapproval of worldly friends; as for hardship, he relished the prospect. But he knew that his mother would be heart-broken. Should he repay her love by deserting her? Could he face wounding one to whom he was devoted? He opened his pocket Bible. A passage in Matthew x seemed to answer his doubts: 'He that loveth father or mother more than me is not worthy of me.' At that he 'knew it was God's wish he should go'.

Studd told no one at the meeting. On the way home, as the two young men sat well wrapped up on the open top of the horse-bus clattering down Essex Road, Studd told Smith that he had 'decided to go to China'.

Stanley Smith was so delighted at the news that on reaching John Street, after parting from Studd, he decided, late as it was, to return to the C. I. M. at Mildmay and break the news to McCarthy and to write to Hudson Taylor, who was away in the country. For Smith and his friends the night of 1st November ended in praise and thanksgiving.

For Studd it ended in conflict. He immediately reported his decision to Kynaston. Kynaston, who knew what it would mean to their mother and who could not forget Charlie's aberrations during the past four months, doubted the validity of the guidance. C. T. broke the news to Mrs. Studd. As he had feared, she was distraught.

The next two days were a nightmare. 'I never saw anything like Kinny's depression,' wrote Monty Beauchamp, who was round there on the Monday night, 3rd November, 'he says he has never in his life seen two such days of suffering and sorrow, referring to his mother. . . . All day she was imploring Charlie not to go up to Mildmay and at all events just to wait one week before giving himself to H. Taylor. He would listen to no entreaties from Mrs. Studd or Kynaston, who looked upon him as a kind of fanatic.' That Monday night Kynaston determined on one last effort: 'Charlie, I think you are making a great mistake. You are away every night at the meetings and don't see your mother. I see her, and this is just breaking her heart.' 'Let us ask God.' replied C. T., 'I don't want to be pig-headed and go out there of my own accord. I just want to do God's will.' J. E. K.'s advice and help had always meant much, and 'it was hard to have him think it was a mistake'. They knelt and put the whole matter in God's hands. 'That night,' said C. T. later, 'I could not get to sleep, but it seemed as though I heard someone say these words over and over, "Ask of me, and I shall give thee the heathen for thine inheritance and the uttermost parts of the earth for thy possession" ' (Ps.2.8).

This verse convinced him. On Tuesday, 4th November, he set his face to Mildmay, called on Hudson Taylor and was accepted. The conflict was not yet over. As, once again, the horse-bus trotted down the dimly-lit Essex Road the entreaties of his brother and his mother's weeping were uppermost in C. T.'s mind. Having held out so long, he was tempted to waver and withdraw his offer to the Mission. He alighted at King's Cross Underground Railway station, and stood on the platform waiting for the Bayswater train to steam in. In despair he prayed for a sure word of guidance. He drew out his pocket Bible. With a platform lamp flickering over his shoulder he opened and read: 'A man's foes shall be they of his own houshold.' With that his way was clear – and when Mrs. Studd knew that C. T. was settled in his decision she withdrew her opposition and supported him warmly for the rest of her life.

Chapter 7

A TORCH IS LIT

C. T. STUDD'S decision influenced a steadily widening circle. The immediate effect was on Montagu Beauchamp. Moody's Cambridge mission, two years earlier, had strengthened Beauchamp's determination to devote his life to Christ. In 1883 he had left Trinity for Ridley Hall, his mind running on ordained service at home. But at the end of the year he began to doubt the reality of his call to ordination, and left Ridley to live in London, spending much time assisting at Moody's meetings, and frequently visiting S. P. Smith at Newlands.

In the summer of '84, for some reason never divulged, his faith suffered severe setback. While C. T. Studd, so long indifferent, was working steadily deeper into wholehearted devotion, Monty Beauchamp was lost in a medley of doubt and spiritual confusion. The whole Beauchamp family rallied to the rescue, determined that Montagu should not be lost to the cause. Early in October their prayers were answered. Monty's eldest sister Ida was the means of bringing him to a 'very deep spiritual experience of reconsecration to God'.

The brief period of backsliding, now that it was over, served to increase Monty's love for the Christ who had not cast him out, and he was determined to discover God's will for his life. Stanley Smith's imminent departure for China was much talked of at the Beauchamp home in South Kensington, but although Monty had as it were acted as broker for the C. I. M. to Hoste, Smith and Arthur Polhill-Turner, he had not previously sensed a personal leading abroad.

On 18th October he met S. P. Smith, fresh from his first farewell tour in Scotland and Ireland, at a young men's meeting at Mildmay. Some days later he happened to see a pamphlet, *A Strange but True Story*, which by a parable presented the claims of the Mission Field so effectively that Beauchamp saw it as a personal challenge.

Ten days afterwards came Studd's sudden decision on 1st November. Hilda Beauchamp had recently become engaged to Kynaston Studd and Montagu was thus drawn close to the family. Kynaston's depression, Mrs. Studd's tears and Charlie's quiet determination sent Beauchamp back to Cromwell Road wondering. He could not help contrasting Mrs. Studd with his own mother. As he wrote to Lady Beauchamp, 'If I am not mistaken I have often heard you say it would be your joy and rejoicing to have a son go to the heathen to "preach the unsearchable riches of Christ" '. If Charlie Studd was willing to go in spite of his family, ought a man hold back whose mother would 'rather encourage than hinder'?

As if to prove that God was behind this trend of thought, Beauchamp, on Monday, 3rd November, down at a 'Holiness meeting' at a Cambridge friend's parish near Shepherd's Bush, met S. P. Smith unexpectedly. They came back together in the Underground and despite the noise, soot and vibration had 'a serious talk about China'. At South Kensington Monty determined to go on with Smith to Victoria, where they had tea in a shop before Smith had to catch a train.

On the Tuesday, while S. P. Smith was enjoying a demure idyll in Richmond Park with Lord Radstock's small daughters and their governess, and C. T. Studd was at Mildmay with Hudson Taylor, Beauchamp went round again to the Studds, where Kynaston poured out his troubles. That night, back in his bedroom at Cromwell Road opposite the new Natural History Museum, Beauchamp studied his Bible and prayed. 'I realized His presence in a way I have never done before,' he told his mother. Earlier that evening God had spoken to C. T. Studd on the station platform; now He spoke to Beauchamp in the quiet of his Kensington home. As Beauchamp read and prayed it was 'made quite clear that not only was I to go but to induce others to go too'. Next morning, when S. P. Smith was shown in by the butler at about eleven o'clock it was to find his tall friend in transports of joy saying he had 'decided to "go into all the world"'.

The same afternoon, 5th November, Smith, Studd and Hoste left for Oxford.

Hoste had retired from the Army in the spring, intending to gain experience by working in Moody's enquiry room. He had written to Hudson Taylor on April 15th, 'not as officially offering myself as a candidate for the C. I. M. , but to let you know how my mind is working in the matter:' he had doubts sometimes, he wrote, but 'my own feeling is that I should go to China, and if so I would esteem [it] a most blessed privilege to go under the auspices of the China Inland Mission.'

Taylor had advised Hoste to get a year's experience in Christian work, but by the autumn both men were sure that nothing need hinder Hoste joining Smith whenever he should leave for China. Hoste was most impressed by Smith, 'Oh *so* attractive! Brilliant fellow,' was his memory in old age. And now they would be accompanied by Studd.

The announcement that Studd was going to China had caused immense excitement in the universities. Not only was C. T. Studd a household name but the suddenness of his decision seemed to make it the more impressive. Smith had been stumping the country for Christ for nearly two years. Studd had been absorbed by cricket. 'We never thought he would go,' was an Eton friend's comment. Moreover his sacrifice, abandoning cricket at the height of his fame, was the more apparent. Oxford undergraduates crowded to hear him on November 6th.

'You have no idea how wonderfully the Lord helped and blessed dear Studd,' wrote Smith to, 'My dear Mr. Hudson Taylor' after the first meeting. 'We were simply so full of the joy of the Lord we could only wear the broadest grin on our faces for the rest of the night!'

They spent six days at Oxford, Beauchamp joining on the Friday and Cassels for the last day. Curiously, in view of what was to happen, the later meetings were not well attended, and at one time Smith and his friends endured a sharp attack of depression and doubt.

At Cambridge, where Smith, Studd and Beauchamp went immediately after, all was different. This was their own University, with a vigorous Christian Union already stirred by Smith's previous visit. Hudson Taylor joined them and a week's mission was planned on behalf of 'China Inland and other parts of the foreign field'.

The effect was marked. As one undergraduate said afterwards, 'We have had missionary meetings and we have been hearing missionaries talk to us from time to time. But when men whom everybody had heard of and many had known personally came up and said "I am going out myself", we were brought face to face with the heathen abroad'.

The opening meeting took place on Wednesday, 12th November, in the Alexandra Hall behind Petty Cury. The Principal of Ridley was in the chair. 'Most remarkable meeting,' wrote Moule afterwards, 'Lord bless it. Deeply moving testimonies.' Hudson Taylor spoke of the joy of surrender 'to a Divine Master who more than satisfies His servants' hearts'. Studd and Beauchamp gave their testimonies, followed by Douglas Hamilton, a young Clare man who hoped in due course to serve in China. Arthur Polhill-Turner also spoke, two years to the day since his conversion at Moody's closing meeting in the great Mission of '82.

The next days were packed with meetings in the colleges and at the Alexandra Hall in the evenings. Smith found time for a scull on the river, sandwiched between personal talks and long stretches of prayer. On Friday he and Studd 'held a watchnight with the Lord from 11 – 6.30 a.m. with a three-quarter hour intermission; a blessed time'.

The next day had 'great power in it'. Hoste and Cassels, who had preached his farewell sermon at South Lambeth the previous weekend, had now come up, though Beauchamp had gone down. On the Sunday afternoon at the Guildhall an open meeting for town and gown was, in Moule's estimation, 'very remarkable'.

Each day enthusiasm was rising. Though some of the dons criticized Smith and Studd for their lack of scholarship, and the more flippant undergraduates wrote them off as eccentric, the Christian Union men were stirred to the depths. Smith won their hearts by his charm and shook them from complacency by the fervour of his call, supported by Studd in clipped, homely phrases. As the men listened to these 'spiritual millionaires', as one undergraduate described them, the very content of the word 'sacrifice' seemed reversed: and each man wondered whether he could afford the cost, not of utter devotion and worldly loss but of compromise and the loss of spiritual power and joy'. Nothing less than the experience of these two men was worth having'.

On the Sunday night, after Smith and Hudson Taylor had spoken, some fifty men rose in their places to signify willingness to serve abroad. On the Monday, Moule took Studd for a walk in the country. Handley Moule, cautious and scholarly, a shrewd judge of character, with a high standard of personal saintliness, found Studd's 'spirit blessed and experience most remarkable'. He was convinced that the hand of God was in the movement. The next night, the last of their visit, came the climax. After a 'grand afternoon of prayer' Studd and Smith spoke at Corpus and then joined the others at a farewell meeting in the Alexandra Hall of a hundred men or more, each a Christian and each anxious to learn God's will for their lives.

At the close, Smith asked 'all who intended to become missionaries' to stay to a prayer meeting. Forty-five stayed. When the time came to close the hall, thirty of them went to a nearby college room to continue in prayer.

One of these thirty was Arthur Polhill-Turner. The course of his life was changed by this week in Cambridge.

During the previous year Polhill-Turner's faith had deepened considerably. At Howbury he found the exacting social round 'hollow and unreal' and preferred with his sister to help the villagers to a share in his spiritual experience. The local vicar would have 'nothing to do with us', but they soon came to know Mrs. Symons and others like her in Ravensden and Renhold, and held meetings in their cottages. Arthur's hopes for his mother were not fulfilled. 'Had a talk with the Mater,' he wrote in his diary on 21st January 1884, 'unsatisfactory; must resort to prayer.' At Cambridge he continued in sport and Christian activities with zest.

Cecil Polhill-Turner of the Bays returned from Germany at the end of March, fresh in his acceptance of Christ. He spent a few days at Howbury, and Arthur soon detected the difference. 'Not an unhappy day since,' was Cecil's own verdict. At Aldershot he gave himself wholeheartedly 'to do my best' for Christ in the drills and exercises, and

the hunting, polo and cricket of a cavalry canton-
ment, though 'racing and card-playing had to be
abandoned, and in many directions a pull-up was
necessary'. He enjoyed the Christian fellowship of
the place, and his fears of ostracism in the Mess
were proved unfounded: 'in view of my eccentrici-
ties, as they thought them, my brother officers
were remarkably considerate . . . a quiet laugh was
occasionally indulged in at my expense, but I must
say I had hardly any ragging to put up with.' He
had shown himself too good an officer to be treated
with disrespect. 'Dear Cecil seemed much grown
in grace and refreshed us by his presence.' wrote
Arthur in August '84 after they had been together at
a Children's Mission on the Bournemouth sands.

Arthur had gone up to Ridley in the Long
Vacation term, his eye still on China. 'My leading
towards the foreign mission field has been very
gradual.' he said later. The first enthusiasm had
been followed by a quiet testing of vocation and
counting the cost. He knew his mother was against
the plan, but that she would let him have his head.
It would not seem hard to leave though the time
was not yet. He set about seeking a curacy, as a
stage on the road abroad, but made no decision.

For the Michaelmas term he was returning to
Cambridge late, and on 27th October took his sister
to Edinburgh for a Convention on Holiness 'with
the desire of receiving blessing for God's glory'.
What Studd and Beauchmp had both received in
London a few weeks earlier Arthur Polhill-Turner
received at Edinburgh, 'very happy times and
seasons of much blessing', discovering, as Smith
had discovered with old Mr. Price at Pakefield, the

secret of consecration and victory and of constant abiding in the power of the Holy Spirit. He came back from Edinburgh to Cambridge, 'asking the Lord to reveal His will'.

Cecil meanwhile, was experiencing a strong sense that God had a plan for him other than the steady rise to a field-marshal's baton. Independently of Arthur he went to a 'China missionary meeting, and from that time I made up my mind to engage in the Lord's work in China'. Despite his desire he was determined to move slowly. 'I could not give up my commission unless sure of my ground, and sure I was doing right and in the Lord's will.' He knew of fine Christian officers whose influence widened as they rose in rank. An older man whom he consulted advised him strongly to stay in the Army, pointing out that the Bays were soon going to India, where the missionary value of Christian officers was incalculable. Furthermore there was the personal cost. Cecil believed that should he become a missionary his uncle, Sir Henry Barron, a Roman Catholic, would cut him out of his will. But to forfeit a fortune seemed trivial beside the unsearchable riches of Christ.

Still feeling an urge to the Far East, Cecil Polhill-Turner called on Hudson Taylor in London for advice. They talked a while, and Hudson Taylor said, 'Let us have some prayer about it', and 'we knelt down', wrote Cecil, 'and just sought the Lord's will'.

All this Arthur knew, when Studd and Smith descended on Cambridge in November. They were staying at Ridley. Polhill-Turner had them to lunch the first day, and was delighted when they invited him to say a few words on his missionary call that evening. He was impressed also when, at the Alexandra Hall, 'Studd testified to receiving the same blessing as I had', and on the following day the three had a 'delightful afternoon of waiting on the Lord (3 hours)'. Arthur realized that Cecil might be joining these four Cambridge men and Hoste. As the meetings proceeded he sensed a challenge that he, too, should join them, and join them at once without waiting for ordination. He had asked God to reveal His will; was this the answer?

The next week, with Smith and Studd gone down but the missionary fervour maintained by a great Church Missionary Meeting with Professor Westcott in the chair, Cecil came up for a three days' visit to Ridley. The two brothers talked and prayed far into the night. Arthur consulted Handley Moule, who strongly disliked the abandonment of ordination training, but was reluctant to dissuade should the Spirit be leading. The burning inward urge to immediate response did not die down. And when the Ridley term ended Arthur Polhill-Turner was reasonably sure it had been his last.

Smith and Studd's Cambridge mission had increased the 'extraordinary interest aroused by the announcement that the captain of the Cambridge eleven and the stroke oar of the Cambridge boat were going out as missionaries'. The news was in everyone's mouth, competing in public interest with the national anxiety for Gordon in Khartoum. These two young men, the world at their feet, seemed to be sacrificing so much so early to bury themselves in the back of beyond on behalf of an obscure interdenominational mission. And, by all accounts, they were doing it with gusto. 'S. P.' and 'C.T.' were daily discovering the depths and heights of grace. 'Dear Charlie is as full of blessing as an egg is of meat,' wrote Smith on 23rd November, while Smith spoke for himself of the 'glorious liberty Christ has won for me'. Both had told Hudson Taylor that their personal wealth was at the Mission's disposal.

Demands for a visit before the two went abroad poured into C.I.M. headquarters. There was little time before the London Farewell booked for 28th November, but they accepted an invitation to Leicester. They spoke, with Hudson Taylor, in the Melbourne Hall, a Baptist centre, on 26th November. It was a crowded meeting, but the man most influenced was the Baptist minister himself, F. B. Meyer, then thirty-seven and unknown. 'Before then,' he wrote afterwards, 'my Christian life had been spasmodic and fitful, now flaming up with enthusiasm, and then pacing wearily over leagues of grey ashes and cold cinders'. He heard the two proclaim their certainty of every Christian's right to victorious living; 'I saw that these young men had something which I had not, but which was within them a constant source of rest and joy.' Next day Meyer was round early at Mrs. Rust's, where the two were staying. He never forgot the scene 'at 7 a.m. in the grey November morning, as daylight was flickering into the bedroom, paling the guttering candles'. Studd and Smith were at their Bibles, wearing their light-blue blazers to keep out the damp. 'You have been up early,' said Meyer. 'Yes,' replied Studd, 'I got up at four. Christ always knows when I have had enough sleep, and He wakes me to have a good time with Him.' As they talked Meyer asked Studd, 'How can I be like you?' 'Have you ever given yourself to Christ, for Christ to fill you?' 'Yes,' replied Meyer, 'I have done so in a general sort of way, but I don't know that I have done it particularly.' 'You must do it particularly also,' the two replied. 'The talk we had then,' wrote Meyer, 'was one of the formative influences of my life,' and while Studd and Smith were back in London the same evening, the future Free Church leader was on his knees alone, until he had yielded the hidden sin which was throttling his ministry.

The Farewell Meeting at the Eccleston Hall near Victoria was duly held on 28th November but it was not to be the end. Hudson Taylor had intended to set off early in January with a miscellaneous party including Hoste, Smith and Cassels. But as his son and daughter-in-law wrote in their biography, 'the unexpected happened, and God's purposes broke in upon these well-laid plans with an over-flowing fulness which carried all before it'.

The human agent was an elderly and noted evangelist living in Liverpool, Reginald Radcliffe, a close friend of Hudson Taylor. Radcliffe had noted Studd's and Smith's influence on students and had a particular desire to extend it to Scotland. With Hudson Taylor's permission he had written to Professor Alexander Simpson of Edinburgh, a distinguished throat specialist and layman, suggesting a visit by the two young men. Earlier in the term at Edinburgh a strong feeling had arisen among the Christians 'that something must be done for our unconverted fellow-students, and accordingly earnest prayer began to rise'. Radcliffe's proposal 'seemed a most direct answer to our prayers'.

On 28th November, Smith and Studd left by the night train from Euston for Glasgow – Studd with nothing but the clothes he stood up in. His mother was very distressed, when Taylor asked her to send a parcel, 'at my son Charlie's erratic movements and going off to Scotland without any clothes of any sort except those he had on. How or why he should wear one shirt night and day till the 9th of December is a mystery to me when he has a supply provided, and one has always been taught that "Cleanliness is next to Godliness" '. She urged Taylor to place him, in China, with an older and sober minded Christian in steady work. 'I feel that he and Mr. Stanley Smith are too much of the same impulsive nature and one excites the other.'

On 2nd December, Studd's twenty-fourth birthday, they spoke to Glasgow University students. Brief visits were then made with Radcliffe to Greenock, Dundee and Aberdeen. 'I have reason to bless the coming of Studd and Stanley Smith.' Studd's host at Aberdeen, Major Ross, told the next General Assembly of the Free Church of Scotland, 'I have been praying for years that God would incline the hearts of my boys to become ministers of the gospel, and he has given me more than I asked. Two of them have, since their visit, decided to become missionaries.'

On Tuesday, 9th December, ten days after their

tour had begun, Studd and Smith arrived in Edinburgh. They had not taken this tour in their stride. 'When we went round the students,' wrote Studd later, 'we were in a mortal funk about meeting them because we had never done anything like this. So we used to stay sometimes all night by the fire on the mat, sometimes praying and sometimes sleeping.' And thus in the meetings, as Smith could write, 'there was much power'.

At Edinburgh all was ready. But even Stanley Smith and C. T. could scarcely have expected the result.

A committee of professors and students had sent sandwich-men tramping the neighbourhood and had circulated printed notices. They had taken the Free Assembly Hall, a large building holding a thousand, and challenged their own faith by announcing that students only would be admitted.

Nevertheless they were afraid. This was the age of strident rationalism; Edinburgh University was largely medical and, despite the impact made by Moody three years earlier, Christianity was at a discount and considered 'only good for psalm-singing and pulling a long face'. 'There were two fears,' said one of the organizers, 'the first – that there would not be a meeting; the second – that if there should be, there would be a "row" – a very common thing amongst Scottish students.'

Studd and Stanley Smith spent the bleak December afternoon in their host's drawing room 'in prayer, till they got victory'.

In the University, as the evening drew on, 'the word went round our class-rooms, "Let us go and give a welcome to the athlete missionaries" '. Well before the hour the hall was crammed. As the committee and speakers knelt in the green-room they could hear the students 'singing their usual before-lecture songs and beating time with their sticks', but Studd shamed the fears of the organizers by calmly thanking God for the result and, as one of them wrote, 'we felt there was going to be a great blessing'.

The two 'athlete missionaries' entered the hall and were warmly cheered. A divinity professor, Dr. Charteris, a Chaplain to the Queen, took the chair. C. T. Studd spoke first, then R. J. Landale, an Oxford man returned from China, and lastly Smith. 'Stanley Smith was eloquent,' one of the students recalled years later, 'but Studd couldn't speak a bit – it was the fact of his devotion to Christ which told, and he, if anything, made the greatest impression.' Again and again he was cheered. 'The fact that a man with such prospects as he should thus devote himself and his fortune gave them an interest in him from the very first,' wrote the chairman. It was an age of ponderous homilies, and by the very contrast of Studd's happy, ungarnished story of spiritual development 'the students were spellbound'.

Landale's talk was on China, and Stanley Smith then began. Taking as his text 'They feared the Lord, and served their own gods', he showed up, 'in words of burning scorn', the flat, effete selfishness which so often passed for Christian service. He was heard in utter stillness. 'As he spoke,' said one of the committee, 'our hearts condemned us.' The atmosphere was tense with spiritual power. Smith swept on, his 'unusual powers of thought, imagination and utterance' roused to highest pitch by the response of his audience.

When he had done, the chairman announced that any who would 'like to shake hands with them and wish them Godspeed' could come forward after the Benediction. The committee expected that few would have sufficient courage in front of other students. To their amazement, 'no sooner had the Benediction been pronounced than there was a stampede to the platform'. Nor was it mere curiosity. 'They were crowding round Studd and Smith to hear more about Christ; deep earnestness was written on the faces of many. . . . It was all so evidently the work of the Holy Spirit.'

The meeting closed and Studd and Smith returned to their host's for a meal before catching the night mail to London. Shortly before half-past ten the two walked down to Waverley Station with a medical professor and several students, who were urging them to return before they left for China'. At the station a hundred students or more were waiting. 'Speech! Speech!' they cried as the two men appeared. Studd stood on a seat and said a few words, resoundingly cheered. The quiet station had seen nothing like it since Gladstone's Midlothian Campaign five years before. A traveller asked what the fuss was about. 'Th're a meedical students,' replied a porter, 'but th're aff their heeds!'

As the train steamed out into the night Smith and Studd were waving from the carriage windows, some of the students running to the end of the platform, cheering and shouting good-bye, while others stood singing 'God be with you till we meet again'.

Chapter 8

SPREADING FIRE

When Stanley Smith and C. T. Studd met again on the afternoon of their return to London, 10th December, 1884, at Kynaston Studd's wedding to Hilda Beauchamp, they were convinced that they should return to Edinburgh. Reginald Radcliffe had an even wider plan: an evangelistic tour through England and Scotland, at which the two young men, with Hudson Taylor, should reach youth with the message which had captivated Edinburgh.

Stanley Smith wrote at once to Hudson Taylor: 'Could you come? And if not, may we go!' It was now, as his son and daughter-in-law wrote, 'becoming clear to Mr. Taylor that the hand of God was in the movement. . . . The whole thing was beginning to stand out before him: the uniqueness of the opportunity and of the band of fellow-workers who had been given him; the evident purpose of the Lord of the Harvest to use them along lines that had always been his own ideal' – concentration on a deepening of spiritual life so that consecration to service would follow. Hudson Taylor agreed willingly to postpone the departure of his recruits but decided that he must go on ahead alone.

The closing three weeks of 1884 were spent in farewells and scattered meetings, and in prayer and consultation with Hudson Taylor. On Christ-

mas Day Smith, Studd and Cassels spoke at the Y.
M. C. A. headquarters in Aldersgate Street before
separating for a last Christmas dinner with their
families. On the 27th Stanley Smith and Monty
Beauchamp took a long walk in Windsor Great Park
and on the 29th Smith, Studd and Cassels were at
Brighton for two meetings arranged by D. E. Hoste.
New Year's Eve was spent with the C. I. M. at
Mildmay. Thus, day by day, humbled by the
evidence of the Holy Spirit's power and their own
inadequacy, the five men were bound closer.

On Friday, 2nd January, 1885, Stanley Smith
went down to Howbury Hall for farewell meetings
in Bedford arranged by the Polhill-Turners. Studd
arrived the following day in time for an 'afternoon
meeting of county people' in the drawing room at
Howbury, some thirty-five neighbours being received by a hostess who found it hard to stomach
her sons' enthusiasm for two eccentric athletes.

Throughout the weekend Cecil and Arthur were
conscious of pull towards immediate service in
China. On the Sunday the four spent a 'quiet
blessed season of prayer', and Smith rejoiced to
sense the brothers' spiritual growth: 'the P-Ts have
come on wonderfully'. By half-past nine on the
Monday morning, trotting back to Howbury in the
wagonette after seeing off Studd and Smith at Bedford Station, Cecil and Arthur were certain of their
call. Before their next guest, a young naval cousin
back from the South Seas, had arrived they had
written to Hudson Taylor. On Thursday, 8th
January, they went up to London to see him 'and
offered ourselves for China', and Hudson Taylor
accepted them, though formalities were not com-

plete until a second interview six days later. Taylor had no doubt that the increase of his Cambridge party to seven was providential and that the Polhill-Turners should go out with the others early in February. In view, however, of the suddenness of their acceptance they agreed to go 'without being formally connected with the Mission, to see the work first', a detail which enabled their mother to speak airily of 'my sons travelling in China', thus hiding from titled and landed friends her disgrace at being the mother of missionaries.

On the evening of 8th January the seven were together for the first time on the platform of the Exeter Hall, supporting Hudson Taylor. Though nothing to what was to come, the hall was 'absolutely packed'. The Polhill-Turners both spoke of their call and Stanley Smith wound up a long meeting with a comparatively short address. From that evening 'the Cambridge Seven' became a household name.

The next day Studd and Smith left Euston by the 1.30 p.m. express for Liverpool. Reginald Radcliffe met them and they began the same evening with a meeting of young men. 'A most remarkable one,' wrote Smith. 'About twelve hundred there – packed: and such a time of power. Many received Jesus. Young men broken down; I hear there were seventy or more awakened. This is the Lord's doing.'

From Liverpool on 10th January, the day that Cecil Polhill-Turner returned to Aldershot and sent in his papers, Studd, Smith and Radcliffe went into Scotland. After a weekend at Aberdeen they moved north to Banff and then south again to the little hill town of Huntly, back through Aberdeen to Montrose and across to Perth. At each, except Huntly, the halls were filled. At Perth, 'about one hundred and fifty stopped to the after-meeting and I believe there were many souls won,' wrote Smith in his diary. On Saturday, 17th January, they drew into Edinburgh.

'This time,' one of the University committee said later, 'our faith was stronger.' They had taken the largest hall in the city, the United Presbyterian Synod Hall. On the Saturday the University Christian Union crowded to a prayer meeting, 'and the spirit of prayer and of power was amongst us in a most wonderful manner. For over one hour one after another rose without a single pause, and we felt that God was going to give a blessing such as we had never seen before'.

On the Sunday afternoon, 18th January, Studd and Smith addressed some thousand 'upper class boys' in the Free Trade Hall, and in the evening they went to the Synod Hall. Nearly two thousand students were awaiting them, 'the largest meeting of students that has ever been held' in Edinburgh. As soon as the two began to speak, 'the old spell was felt, and the ever-new blessing was experienced'. The purpose was now frankly evangelistic'. 'I lifted up Christ crucified,' wrote Smith simply, 'and Charlie gave his testimony.' None there could afterwards forget, as Dr. Moxey of the divinity faculty wrote, Smith's 'big muscular hands and long arms stretched out in entreaty while he eloquently told out the old story of redeeming love', or Studd's 'quiet but intense and burning utterances of personal testimony to the love and power of a personal Saviour'. After Reginald Radcliffe had closed with a 'fervant appeal for men to consecrate themselves to the service of God', those who wished to do so were invited to stay to an after-meeting. More than half the hall stayed, and when a few more words had been spoken from the platform, Studd and Smith and their helpers went down to the body of the hall, which 'was covered with men anxious about their souls'. 'We spent the time in talking with the dear fellows,' wrote Smith, 'who seemed to drink in the Word.'

On the Monday morning a succession of students crossed Princes Gardens to call at 50 Queen Street where Studd and Smith were staying, 'for interviews restricted to a quarter of an hour'. 'Well, are you a Christian?' Studd would ask each one. 'No'. 'Would you like to be one?' 'Yes.'. . . In the afternoon a general meeting was held in the Free Assembly Hall, with Horatius Bonar, the great hymnodist, in the chair, and the students were back again for an extra meeting in the evening. Once again a crowded hall listened in stillness, 'a large proportion stopping to the after-meeting; we had some precious conversations after,' wrote Smith, 'and some deep work was done. Went home late and stopped with an anxious soul till about 1 a.m.'

It was now clear that the Spirit of God was moving, and that the 'two young athletes from Cambridge' had, as Dr. Moxey wrote, 'precipitated a shower of blessing'. They were due on Clydeside on the Tuesday. Professor Greenfield and John Thomson, a senior student, saw them off at Princes Street Station. 'To the men whom God had so signally used we said, "Can you not possibly come back?" ' All they could offer was to break their journey on the Friday, travelling on to Newcastle, their next engagement, early on Saturday.

The Glasgow neighbourhood echoed Edinburgh. 'God came down in power,' wrote Smith, and it was small wonder that on the first night they 'came home singing and rejoicing'. There were no meetings in the city, but at Greenock, Rutherglen and at Alexandria in Dunbartonshire people of all classes overflowed the kirks and halls. On the Thursday morning, staying with a wealthy young business man at Alexandria, they slept late, but soon they were hard at work again. 'God came down mightily. Souls converted and delivered. . . . God fell on the audience. Many got definite soul blessing.' Smith was not given to exaggeration.

On the Friday, as promised, they were back in Edinburgh. One of the organizers, wrote Smith, 'met our cab and told us good news of the students'. All the signs of true religious revival were about. The meetings had not proved a flash in the pan; men converted on the Sunday were seeking out their friends on the Monday and bringing them to Christ.

That night, after a prayer meeting at midday and dinner (with a short address afterwards) at the Free Church theological college, Studd and Smith went to 'the last meeting with the students and perhaps the most remarkable'. 'I think I never saw a meeting like that', John Thomson told the C. I. M. six months later. Many were in tears before the end, and three or four hundred stayed to the after-meeting. At half past ten the floor was still 'covered with men anxiously enquiring "What must I do to be saved?" ' One of the committee sought out the manager and obtained an extension of lease till midnight, and up to the end could be seen 'the glorious sight of professors dealing with students and students with one another'. As for Smith and Studd, they were utterly humbled. 'There were several conversions.' was all Smith could find in him to say, 'and many began to yield to God what had long been His due.'

Newcastle, Manchester, Rochdale, Leeds – through the smoke-grimed cities of the North, Smith and Studd moved in a triumphal tour, though the triumph was not theirs but Christ's. At Manchester on 26th January, 'a most glorious meeting,' wrote Stanley Smith, 'nearly all young men. Fully a thousand stayed to the after-meeting: and going away we did have our hands squeezed, a somewhat painful show of friendship!' At Rochdale, the next day, they had 'a most remarkable meeting. Quite the most remarkable.' Studd's comment was more picturesque. 'We had a huge after-meeting.' he wrote to his mother, 'it was like a charge of dynamite exploded among them.'

Wherever they went the effect was the same. Young men of all classes flocked to hear them. In the early 'eighties wealth and position could command a respect untinged with envy, while the testimony of the greatest all-round cricketer in England, supported by a prominent oarsman, could impress where other men's words fell flat. And because of the imminent sacrifice of all that the world held dear, many could take from Studd and Smith what they would not from older men whose calling, however rightly, was conducted from cosy vicarages. Studd and Smith were the men for the hour.

They knew well enough that they were neither better nor more important than other Christian workers, but because they had yielded all they were given all. 'I cannot tell you how very much the Lord has blessed us,' wrote Studd to his mother, 'and we daily grow in the knowledge of Jesus and His wonderful love; what a different life from my former one; why, cricket and racquets and shooting are nothing to this overwhelming joy.' Furthermore, their conscience was stirred to the depths by the North, still in the throes of the industrial depression of the early 'eighties. 'Finding out so much about the poor in the great towns,' wrote Studd, 'has increased my horror at the luxurious way I have been living; so many suits and clothes of all sorts, whilst thousands are starving and perishing of cold, so all must be sold when I come home if they have not been so before.'

On Thursday, 29th January, Studd, Smith and Radcliffe came back where they had started a fortnight before, reaching Liverpool early in the afternoon. After a brief rest at the Radcliffes', out at Waterloo, they came in for the final meeting at the Y. M. C. A. 'Packed, and an overflow pretty full.' The two were told afterwards that sixty young men had 'professed conversion on that one night'.

Shortly before eleven the two jumped into a cab for Lime Street Station. Symbolically, at the end of such a whirlwind tour, the cab horse 'ran away with us' and bolted down Pembroke Place, though fortunately no damage was done'

After reaching London in a cheerless drizzle in the dark of the early morning, and spending the day quietly at their homes, Stanley Smith and C. T. Studd joined the others on the evening of Friday, 30th January, for the C. I. M.'s final London Farewell at the Eccleston Hall. Hudson Taylor had left England the previous week.

From then on, except for a rushed visit by Studd and Smith at the weekend to Bristol, where the Colston Hall was not large enough for those who came to hear them, the Cambridge Seven were together. The C.I.M. had arranged a meeting at Cambridge and another at Oxford and had agreed to postpone the Seven's departure one further day, at the urgent request of the Y. M. C. A., for a last public meeting at Exeter Hall in the Strand, the historic rendezvous of evangelicals, which the Y. M. C. A. had recently bought and refurbished.

These three meetings burned the message of the Seven into the consciousness of the nation.

'When before,' asked one religious newspaper, 'were the stroke of a University eight, the captain of a University eleven, an officer of the Royal Artillery, an officer of the Dragoon Guards, seen standing side by side renouncing the careers in which they had already gained no small distinction, putting aside the splendid prizes of earthly ambition. . . and plunging into that warfare whose splendours are seen only by faith and whose rewards seem so shadowy to the unopened vision of ordinary men?' Yet the crowds did not come to

flatter or gape. 'Spirituality,' recalled Eugene Stock
of the C. M. S.,'marked most emphatically the
densely crowded meetings at which these seven
men said farewell. They told, modestly and yet
fearlessly, of the Lord's goodness to them, and of
the joy of serving Him; and they appealed to young
men, not for their Mission, but for the divine
Master.'

The Cambridge Seven attracted not only by their
birth and athletic prowess, and by the sacrifice
they were evidently making, but because they
were not cut to a pattern. Smith and Studd were
ascetics, reacting violently from the comfort of their
early lives. The Polhill-Turners, no less devoted,
did not make such sharp distinctions. 'C. T. believed in rigid austerity,' wrote Cecil Polhill later,
describing a journey in China, 'and no comfort of
any sort, either of furniture or luxury in food were
for a moment allowed. He would not allow himself
even a back to a chair. My brother was mildly
aesthetic. . . . To me it did not matter one way or
the other, all was good, and so we hit it off capi-
tally.' Hoste and Cassels were both fastidious men,
though going to the squalor of China with as much
readiness as Cassels had gone to the slums.

At first meeting Smith would seem severe,
though affectionate and charming on closer ac-
quaintance, but Studd's gentleness almost belied
his burning words. Beauchamp, with his enormous frame and somewhat florid face and his
capacity to extract enjoyment from anything, was
almost as eloquent as Smith; but Hoste and Cecil
Polhill-Turner were shy and found public speaking
a trial. Cassels, as quiet as Hoste, as good a speaker

as Beauchamp, was in many ways the most mature of them all.

The Cambridge farewell took place in the Guildhall at 8 p.m. on Monday, 2nd February. 'Very soon after 7.30' wrote the *Record* 'the great hall was crowded in every corner – floor, orchestra, gallery. Quite twelve hundred persons must have been present, including a very large number of gownsmen.' Professor Babington, an ancient botanist, was in the chair. The Seven had asked for him 'because', they told Moule, 'he is so large hearted, he loves all who love the Lord Jesus Christ', and his presence, commented the *Record*, was a 'valuable testimonial of confidence in a devoted, spiritual enterprise on the part of a leading representative of science.' Another testimony had come from the eminent classical scholar and headmaster, J. .H. Moulton, who had told Benjamin Broomhall, Hudson Taylor's brother-in-law and secretary of the C. I. M., that he regarded the going out of the Seven 'as a most remarkable thing in itself and in its influence on the University.'

After Babington and Broomhall and two serving missionaries had spoken, Stanley Smith took the platform. 'Mr. Stanley Smith,' reported the *Cambridge Review*, 'gave an earnest address, delivered with great fervour listened to with the closest attention. He spoke of the great love of God and their duty to the Saviour. Nothing had won their heart so much as the love of Christ upon the Cross. The theme they had come to dwell upon that night was, "God so loved the world".' Exhorting them all to let their hearts 'extend and go out to the world', he closed with an impassioned warning that 'unless we spread abroad the light we will find in England, as elsewhere, that we cannot hold our own with the powers of darkness'.

Beauchmp spoke next, followed by Hoste and the others, 'with very different degrees of eloquence but with beautifully uniform simplicity in stating their motive and hope, and confessing their Lord's name and claims'. Studd told, as so often before, the simple story of his call. 'He was first led to give up cricket,' reported the papers, 'as he felt he had got a possession far greater, although he had before such a love for cricket that he did not believe any man had greater in this world, and finally he was led to give himself wholly to God's service.' His closing words were long remembered: 'What I would have you gather is that God does not deal with you until you are wholly given up to Him, and then He will tell you what He would have you do.'

A brief word from Cassels, an expression of thanks to the chairman, a closing prayer, and the great meeting broke up quietly. Moule felt it had been 'the most remarkable missionary meeting held within living memory at Cambridge . . . it has stirred hearts deeply far and wide'. An 'enthusiastic packed meeting' was Smith's comment, but the enthusiasm was quiet and spiritual. 'After the meeting,' said J. C. Farthing of Caius, later a missionary and bishop, 'I went back to my rooms and thought of the words I had heard. I saw this: that we were to take up our cross and follow Christ; that there was to be no compromise, however small; that there was to be nothing between us and our

Master; that we were to be wholly for Christ.'

The Seven went on to Oxford, where on the next night, Tuesday, 3rd February, the Corn Exchange, the largest hall in the city, was filled to overflowing, with many standing, though the proportion of undergraduates was less. Smith arrived late, having broken his journey to say good-bye to one of his brothers, but he and all the Seven took part and the meeting was described as 'of almost unparalleled interest'.

The next morning the Seven returned to London for their last day in England, closing in no uncertain manner with the meeting in Exeter Hall.

Chapter 9

INEXTINGUISHABLE BLAZE

'*Exeter Hall* – last night, what shall I say? Such a meeting!' wrote Benjamin Broomhall to Hudson Taylor next morning. 'I question if a meeting of equal significance and spiritual fruitfulness has been held in that building during this generation. Its influence upon the cause of missions must be immense, incalculable.'

'It was a most magnificent success,' he went on. 'Exeter Hall was packed in every part and people of note and title had to get in anywhere and be thankful if they got in at all. . . That meeting will be the talk of all England wherever men meet who are interested in the cause of missions.'

Rain had been falling hard all evening, but 'long before the time announced', reported *The Times*, 'the large hall was crowded in every part, and an overflow meeting of some of the many unable to obtain admission was held in the small hall'. 'Over three thousand,' Stanley Smith was told, 'and the overflow five hundred, besides hundreds going away.' Dr. Barnardo and other well-known figures had to stand the entire time.

The meeting had been arranged for young men but they were lost in a miscellaneous mass of men and women 'of all sections of the Church and grades of social life'. Smith's parents were there. Lady Beauchamp squeezed in beside her daughter at the organ. Mrs. Studd came with Kynaston and his wife, Monty's sister. Mrs. Polhill-Turner, still faintly disapproving, had brought her three daughters. Only Mrs. Cassels was unable to face it. 'May God not despise the feebleness of my faith in giving you,' she had written to William, 'and may we still not feel separate, but meet together before the Throne of Grace. . . . I cannot tell you all I feel for you.'

When George Williams, founder of the Y. M. C. A., entered to take the chair, 'every nook and corner where a human being could sit or stand was crowded', while behind him, beneath the vast map of China, were forty Cambridge undergraduates, all intending missionaries. As the Seven filed in 'they were received', said *The Times*, 'with great enthusiasm'. Though a religious meeting there was round upon round of cheering and clapping, to be succeeded by silence the moment George Williams raised his hand.

An Anglican clergyman opened with prayer and the hall resounded with the missionary hymn, 'Tell it out among the heathen that the Lord is King'. When all were seated again George Williams presented each of the Seven with a Chinese New Testament on behalf of the British and Foreign Bible Society, 'as a memento of this great occasion'. Benjamin Broomhall spoke briefly of the work of the China Inland Mission, followed, as at Cambridge, by R. J. Landale. And then, one by one, it was the turn of the Seven. 'A sight to stir the blood,' wrote the *Nonconformist*, 'and a striking testimony to the power of the uplifted Christ to draw to

112

Himself not the weak, the emotional, the illiterate only but all that is noblest in strength and finest in culture.'

Stanley Smith spoke first and longest. Taking a text from the eleventh chapter of Proverbs, 'There is that scattereth, and yet increaseth; and there is that withholdeth more than is meet, but it tendeth to poverty', he delivered a remarkable address which held the audience spellbound. 'I suppose we all allow,' he began, 'that we are under obligation to spread the knowledge of a good thing. It is this simple fact, coupled with our having heard the clear note of the Master's call, which is sending us out from England's shores. We do not go to that far distant field to speak of doctrine or theory, but of a living, bright, present and rejoicing Saviour.' The Apostles and their converts of old did not go out to propagate 'the milk-and-water of religion but the cream of the Gospel, and to tell what a blessed thing it was to have the love of the Lord Jesus Christ reigning in their hearts. This, dear friends, is the Gospel we want to recommend. We want to go to the Chinaman, buried in theories and prejudices, and bound by the chains of lust, and say, "My brother, I bring to you an Almighty Saviour".'

Soon Smith was turning the minds of his listeners to their own responsibility. 'Let us try and take a bird's-eye view of *this world*. . . . I would just call your attention to this fact, that the knowledge of this precious Jesus, who, I hope to most of us, is everything in the world, is absolutely wanting to thousands and millions of our brethren and sisters to the present day. What are we going to

113

do? What is the use of calling big meetings like this if the outcome is not to be something worthy of the name of Jesus?'

One by one he conjured vivid pictures which lit up his argument: he described the feeding of the Five Thousand as if it was taking place in the hall, and the disciples distributing the food. 'But at the end of the eighth row they stop and turn back to the first and feed these eight rows again, pouring bread and fish into their laps and piling it about them. . . . What do you suppose our Lord would say? He would say, What are you doing? Here, Andrew, Peter, John, what are you doing? Don't you see the starving multitudes behind? . . . ' William Carey the cobbler, first Protestant missionary, Arnott waking across Africa, Livingstone, buried with crowds and ceremonial in Westminster Abbey: 'If Livingstone could leap to life, what would he say? "Do not follow my body home to this cathedral, but follow where my heart lies, out yonder in Africa." '

Smith touched the emotion of the hour with reference to Gordon, none then knowing that Khartoum had fallen. 'Oh, to think that Gordon has but to speak a word from Khartoum and millions of money go from England. But a greater than Gordon cries from Khartoum. . . . The voice of Christ from the Cross of Calvary.'

In profound stillness he reached his peroration. 'And now one last word. How can one leave such an audience as this? It seems to me as if Christ has come right into your midst, and has looked into the face of you men and women, young, old and middle-aged. He would take hold with loving hands of each one, and looking into your eyes point to the wounds in His pierced side, and ask "Lovest thou me?" And you would say, "Yea, Lord, thou knowest that I love thee." And what is the test of love? "If you love me keep my commandments." And what, Master, do you command? "Go ye into all the world and preach the gospel to every creature." '

Montagu Beauchamp rose, while Smith slipped away to the overflow meeting which Studd and some of the others had already addressed. Beauchamp spoke more briefly, followed by Hoste, who said, 'I stand here for the first time in my life, and, I suppose, for the last time, to address an audience of such size,' and asked them all 'to pray that God may keep us faithful'. Cassels spoke longer, and then Cecil Polhill-Turner. His resignation was not yet gazetted and he could still be introduced as 'of the 2nd Dragoon Guards', with all the glamour implied to a Victorian audience by a crack cavalry commission. He spoke only five sentences, saying he had 'found the greatest peace and happiness by resting my soul on the Lord, and I recommend all of you to do the same'.

Young Arthur Polhill-Turner, three days short of his twenty-third birthday, spoke sixth, as briefly as his brother, followed by J. C. Farthing on behalf of the Cambridge undergraduates.

C. T. Studd then rose. 'I want to recommend you tonight to my Master,' he began, 'I have tried many ways of pleasure in my time; I have been running after the best master – and, thank God, I have found Him.' Unhurriedly, without flourish or effect, he told the story of 'how the Lord has sought and found me and led me back to Himself.' The simplicity of the narrative, coming from such a man as Studd, brought the challenge of Christ to every man and woman present. 'What are you really living for?' he concluded, 'Are you living for the day or are you living for the life eternal? Are you going to care for the opinion of men here, or for the opinion of God? The opinion of men won't avail us much when we get before the judgement throne. But the opinion of God will. Had we not, then, better take His word and implicitly obey it?'

Over two hours had passed. Hugh Price Hughes, the great Nonconformist, who was to give the closing address, leant across to the chairman and suggested that 'at this late hour' he should not speak. But the audience showed no restlessness. George Williams told him to carry on, and Hughes concluded the meeting with a rousing word of encouragement to the Seven, to the China Inland Mission and to all who would consecrate themselves to God:'if every man and woman here present would come now and offer themselves to God a living sacrifice, what an enormous power of good they would effect.' In words which proved prophetic he added, 'There is enough power in this meeting to stir not only London and England but the whole world.'

The audience rose. After a final prayer the organ struck up Mozart's tune, and in Frances Ridley Havergal's Consecration Hymn the whole hall echoed the sentiments which had been heard and felt. Verse by verse, each more stirring than the last, they reached the climax of sober dedication:

'Take my love, my Lord, I pour
At Thy feet its treasure store.
Take myself, and I will be
Ever, only, all for Thee.'

Soon after half-past nine the next morning, 5th
February, 1885, the Seven were at Victoria Station.
Relations and friends were there in plenty. Lady
Beauchamp, and Kynaston Studd and his wife,
were to travel as far as Calais. Studd's popularity
had drawn several of the M. C. C. team.

They stood about in desultory conversation, discussing the rumours of Gordon's death, confirmed
later that morning, giving each other last-minute
messages, recalling incidents of the previous night.
'An affecting time,' as Stanley Smith said, 'I could
hardly believe I was going off.'

Carriage doors were shut, a whistle blew, and at
10 a.m. the Boat Train drew slowly out. The Cambridge Seven were on their way to Dover and
Calais, Brindisi, Suez, Colombo and China.

EPILOGUE

The Cambridge Seven arrived at Shanghai on 18th
March, 1885. On board ship and at meetings in
ports, and in the International Settlement before
they went up country, their effect was no less remarkable than at home. Their fame had preceded
them and they turned it to Christ's account.

Behind them in Britain their influence increased.
The interest was enormous. 'In one short week,'
wrote Benjamin Broomhall, 'the China Inland
Mission has been suddenly lifted into unusual and
unexpected prominence, and even popularity.'
Fifty thousand copies were sold of the issue of
China's millions which reported the farewell meetings. A year later, from these reports and letters
from the Seven, with much matter on the worldwide mission field, Broomhall compiled *A Missionary Band*, which at once became a best-seller.

At Edinburgh a series of evangelistic meetings,
chaired by Professor Drummond, the scientist,
'became more and more crowded'. Groups of
students, led by professors, spread out across Scotland carrying the revival to universities and towns.
When David Cairns, the theologian, then a young
man, returned in 1886 after six years abroad he
found the whole atmosphere changed and the
theological colleges full. At Cambridge Handley

Moule was soon finding it 'constantly my duty at Ridley Hall to press urgently on men the claims of the home field, so almost universal was the longing to serve the Lord in the end of the unevangelized world.'

In the United States the interest was no less. In the summer of 1885 J. E. K. Studd visited American universities at Moody's invitation, receiving a great welcome as brother of one of the Seven. Studd's tour and the wide circulation of *A Missionary Band* led directly to the formation of the Student Missionary Volunteers at the Mount Hermon Conference in Massachusetts in '86. That autumn Robert Wilder and R. S. Forman, fired by the Seven's example, toured the American campus, drawing in over two thousand missionary volunteers in a year.

Robert Wilder brought the Volunteer Movement to Britain in 1891. And thus, through the Student Volunteer Missionary Union of Great Britain, formed early in 1892, the Cambridge Seven were ancestors of the Student Christian Movement, and later of the Inter-Varsity Fellowship,– now the Universities and Colleges Christian Fellowship (in Britain) and the Inter-Varsity Christian Fellowship (in the United States). These two were among the founders of the International Fellowship of Evangelical Students which, by the Centenary year of the Cambridge Seven, linked students in a hundred countries across the world, a Chinese Christian being the general secretary.

At Cambridge itself the fame of the Seven never faded. Their seventieth anniversary in 1955 inspired the Christian Union to pray for a Cambridge Seventy to 'serve the Lord overseas.'

Almost seventy of that generation did in fact go.

Not one of the Cambridge Seven looked back, and a high proportion of their children (all the seven married) became missionaries in their turn.

The paths of the Seven diverged. William Cassels, developing the pastoral gifts he had shown, worked first in Shansi and later in the West. In 1895, during his first furlough, he was consecrated, at the age of thirty-six, Bishop of the new diocese of Western China, where he remained with infrequent leaves until his death in 1925, the first of the Seven to die.

Both Stanley Smith and C. T. Studd died in 1931. Smith's life was spent in North China. He became a fine linguist and as fluent a preacher in Chinese as in English. In 1902 he left the C. I. M. because he adopted views on the ultimate destiny of unbelievers which were unacceptable to colleagues. The aged Hudson Taylor would have liked him to remain in the Mission, and the controversy was conducted in a most loving spirit, but he worked thenceforth as an independent in Eastern Shansi. His name was forgotten by the public though his son Geoffrey Stanley-Smith became well known as a medical missionary in Ruanda, East Africa.

Stanley in later years endured severe trials and disappointments but worked on until the end, preaching and teaching (and writing up his diary) until the night before he died, at Tse-Chow on 31st January, 1931.

C. T. Studd was the best known of the Seven in later life. His courage and endurance were unquenchable. In 1887, determined to live by faith alone, he gave away the whole of his fortune. His mother and family disapproved but when he married and had four daughters, they nobly paid for their education.

In 1894, broken in health, Studd and his wife left China, never to return. After six years in India and a period in Britain and America, where his words did much for the missionary cause, Studd set off in 1910 into the depths of tropical Africa, pioneering in defiance of illness, criticism and poverty. 'C. T.'s life stands as some rugged Gibraltar,' wrote his son-in-law and companion, Alfred Buxton, 'an eternal rebuke to easy-going Christianity.' from his faith grew the Heart of Africa Mission and the Worldwide Evangelization Crusade, and though in later years he became a controversial figure, nothing could detract from the splendour of C. T. Studd's witness to Christ. Studd died at Ibambi, Belgian Congo, on 16th July 1931, over a thousand Africans seeing him to his grave. His biography by his son-in-law, Norman Grubb made his story known worldwide.

The Polhill-Turners' lives were less spectacular. Arthur Polhill (they dropped their second name), having left his theological course unfinished to join the Seven, was ordained in China in 1888. For ten years he lived in Pachow in North Szechwan, later moving to other stations in the province, using them as bases for evangelism in the thickly populated countryside. He was in China throughout the Boxer Rising and the Revolution of 1911, and not until 1928, at the age of sixty-six, did he retire. He took a country living in Hertfordshire, and died in 1935.

Cecil Polhill, after a short while in Shansi, moved steadily north-west, set on reaching the forbidden land of Tibet. He became great friends with the Tibetans in Kansu, and made contact through travellers with the Dalai Lama. Moving south to Sungpan in Western Szechwan, still bordering Tibet, Cecil Polhill and his wife almost lost their lives in a violent riot in 1892. After recovering health by a visit to England they spent nearly a year on the Tibetan border of India before returning to China. Again they went to the Tibetan border. In 1900, withdrawn to the coast with all other missionaries during the Boxer Rising, Cecil Polhill was invalided home, and the doctors forbade permanent return. In 1903 he inherited Howbury Hall, but his heart was in China and he made seven prolonged missionary visits. 'The Lord make us to be inextinguishable firebrands,' was his prayer, 'so that no matter how cold the reception of our message may be, the fire may burn on and on.' He died at Howbury in 1938 in his eightieth year.

Montagu Beauchamp was the itinerant member of the Seven. He loved the hard evangelistic journeys. With Hudson Taylor he once went, as he wrote, 'about a thousand miles in intense heat, walking through market towns and villages, living in Chinese inns and preaching the gospel to crowds day by day'. He always carried either a scroll or a large palm leaf fan attached to a stick, inscribed in big characters, *Repent, the Kingdom of Heaven is at hand*.

His eldest brother, who had no son, offered Montagu a substantial share in his fortune if he would return to help run the Norfolk estate. This he refused. Evacuated in the Rising of 1900 Beauchamp was in China again in 1902, until final return in 1911.

In England he was ordained. After a few years' parish work he became a Chaplain to the Forces in the Great War, serving in Egypt and Greece and ending the war as Senior Chaplain at Murmansk in North Russia. He had inherited the baronetcy when his next elder brother was killed in action in Gallipoli on the same day as his own eldest son. In 1929, Sir Montagu revisited China, where his second son was starting work with the C. I. M., and toured extensively, and again in 1935, physically as strong and untiring as ever.

In 1939, aged 79, he joined a party of missionary recruits driving overland through French Indo-China via Hanoi to Chungking, but he was already suffering from cancer, and died at his son's station, Paoning, in October 1939.

D. E. Hoste worked with the famous Pastor Hsi in Shansi until 1896. A man of great prayerfulness, as wise as he was gentle, Hoste was appointed Acting General Director of the C. I. M. in 1901, succeeding Hudson Taylor as its head in 1903. He became an outstanding missionary statesman, though never one to hit the headlines , and led the Mission for over thirty years. Despite revolution, civil war and anti-foreign agitation its strength rose from 716 on the active list when he took over, to 1326 when he retired.

Hoste remained in Shanghai and in 1944 was

interned by the Japanese, leaving China in October 1945, weak and aged, more than sixty years after his arrival. He died in London, last of the Cambridge Seven, in May 1946.

Long after the later lives of the men who formed it are forgotten the Cambridge Seven, will remain in the consciousness of the Christian Church. Their social background, in an aristocratic age, and their athletic prowess at a time when organized games were first becoming popular, ensured them the widest hearing. Their refusal to be content with the formal piety which characterized their class endeared them to the masses, for whom religion was still the core of existence.

Later generations may detect in them defects of their period: they did not happen to be scholars and, since they were never likely to be dependent on educational attainments for their livelihood, they saw no cause to take academic work more seriously than most undergraduates of the eighteen-eighties. Again they were not without social conscience but theories of social reorganization were almost unknown and it was not strange that the Seven should have taken extremes of poverty and wealth for granted. And if they seem to have been at times over-exuberant in word and action, they lived in a colourful and demonstrative age.

Beside such criticisms must be placed the splendid sacrifice of the Seven, their wholehearted devotion to the call of Christ, their intolerance of shoddy spirituality in themselves or in others, and their grasp of the urgency of the gospel to unevangelized millions overseas. And, particularly relevant, not one of the Seven was a genius. Theirs is a story of ordinary men, and thus may be repeated, not only in countries of the West but in lands which were the mission fields of a century ago but now send missionaries themselves.

The gospel of Christ is unchanged and His call is unchanged. The Cambridge Seven illustrate how that call may be heard. It is a call to 'lift up your eyes and look on the fields, for they are white already to harvest'. It is a call to dedication. Above all it is a call to the consecration of the whole man, as the prelude to fruitful service.

The message of the Cambridge Seven echoes down the years from 1885: 'God does not deal with you until you are wholly given up to Him, and then He will tell you what He would have you do.

MANUSCRIPT SOURCES

The Hudson Taylor Papers (Archives of the China Inland Mission—Overseas Missionary Fellowship)

The Diaries of Stanley Smith, 1879–85.

Arthur Polhill-Turner's Diary, 1884–5.

Two Etonians in China, unpublished reminiscences of Cecil and Arthur Polhill.

Letters and Papers of Sir Montagu Beauchamp, Bt.

FOR FURTHER READING

Bishop Cassels, by Marshall Broomhall, C.I.M., 1926.

D. E. Hoste, by Phyllis Thompson, C.I.M., 1948.

C. T. Studd: Cricketer and Pioneer, by Norman Grubb, Lutterworth Press, 1933.

A Missionary Band, edited by B. Broomhall, Morgan & Scott, 1886.

Hudson Taylor and the China Inland Mission, by Dr. and Mrs. Howard Taylor, C.I.M., 1918.

A Cambridge Movement, by J. C. Pollock, John Murray, 1953.

Hudson Taylor and Maria, by John Pollock, Hodder and Stoughton 1962, Reissued Kingsway 1983 (Zondervan in USA)

Moody Without Sankey, by John Pollock, Hodder and Stoughton, 1963, Reissued 1983. (Moody Press in USA)

Hudson Taylor and China's Open Century, by A. J. Broomhall, 6 volumes, Hodder and Stoughton and Overseas Missionary Fellowships, 1981—.

A Passion For the Impossible, The Centenary History of the China Inland Mission, by Leslie Lyall, Hodder and Stoughton, 1965.